Road to Box Office

Road to Box Office

*The Seven Film Comedies
of Bing Crosby, Bob Hope and
Dorothy Lamour, 1940–1962*

by

Randall G. Mielke

McFarland & Company, Inc., Publishers
Jefferson, North Carolina, and London

Frontispiece: Bing Crosby, Dorothy Lamour and Bob Hope pose for a publicity photo for their 1952 film *Road to Bali.*

British Library Cataloguing-in-Publication data are available

Library of Congress Cataloguing-in-Publication Data

Mielke, Randall G.
    Road to box office : the seven film comedies of Bing Crosby, Bob
Hope and Dorothy Lamour, 1940–1962 / by Randall G. Mielke.
       p.   cm.
    Filmography: p.
    Includes bibliographical references and index.
    ISBN 0-7864-0162-1 (library binding : 50# alkaline paper) ∞
    1. Crosby, Bing, 1904–1977. 2. Hope, Bob, 1903–   . 3. Lamour,
Dorothy, 1914–1996. 4. Motion picture actors and actresses—United
States—Biography. I. Title.
PN2287.C6826M54   1997
791.43'617—dc21   96-52179
                                                 CIP

Manufactured in the United States of America

McFarland & Company, Inc., Publishers
  Box 611, Jefferson, North Carolina 28640

To my mother,
who taught me how to travel the road of life

Contents

Preface

Author Toni Morrison once said, "If there's a book you really want to read, but it hasn't been written yet, then you must write it." I decided to do just that.

The idea for a book about the "Road" pictures began when I was a child growing up in the late 1950s and early 1960s. As I watched old movies on television, I found that my tastes gravitated towards comedies and musicals. These TV versions of the motion pictures that had originally been shown in theaters in the 1930s and 1940s were always heavily edited and reduced in running time to fit certain TV time slots. This meant that I never got the total effect of seeing them on a full-sized motion picture screen or in their entirety. Still, I enjoyed these old films and watched as many as I could.

As I grew older and found the wonder of books in libraries and book stores, I would seek out volumes on my favorite topics. Over the years these topics ranged from auto racing and ice hockey to plays and movies. One movie genre that particularly appealed to me was the comedic film laced with music. In the books at the library, I was able to find out more about a particular film than I would have known by simply watching it. By looking up specific films in reference books, I was able to deduce that songs or scenes might have been eliminated from the versions I had seen.

What I did not find in the hallowed halls of reading rooms was a book that covered a particular series of films with which I had fallen in love. There were no volumes on the "Road" pictures of Bing Crosby, Bob Hope, and Dorothy Lamour. Later, when I became a professional writer, I thought that writing a book on the subject might be in order.

During the course of writing this book, I again turned to libraries for research. In addition to the regular books from which I collected information (a list of which appears in the bibliography), I attempted to find as many listings of cast and credits as possible.

My telephone and letter inquiries led me from coast to coast. On the East Coast, I contacted the New York Public Library for Performing Arts and the Library of Congress Motion Picture Broadcasting and Sound Division in Washington, D.C. On the West Coast, I was in touch with the special collection libraries at the University of Southern California and the University of California–Los Angeles.

Although these contacts provided some information, invariably my inquiries brought me back to one source: the Margaret Herrick Library of the Academy of Motion Picture Arts and Sciences in California.

As a result, the cast and crew credits for most of the films are extensive. If there are certain elements lacking in some of the credits, it is probably because records of these credits no longer exist. As several reference librarians informed me, although films are often saved, much of the background material on the films is simply destroyed or discarded. Although these credits are not as balanced as I would have liked, with some films having more credits than others, I believe the "Road" credits are as complete as they can be.

Of the many people who helped with this project, several must be singled out.

First and foremost, I would like to thank Timm Boyle for his extensive work and helpful editing throughout the various stages of the manuscript. For this, and for his continued advice and support, I will always be grateful.

I also would like to thank Jim Suva for his help with some of the research on this book. In addition, I am grateful for his encouragement during the times when the project sometimes got me down.

Special thanks go to Janet Lorenz of the National Film Information Service of the aforementioned Margaret Herrick Library of the Academy of Motion Picture Arts and Sciences. She was very instrumental in my obtaining a majority of the credits and cast listings of the "Road" pictures.

And, as always, thanks to my friends and my family, who have supported me in this and all my endeavors. I love you all.

And, finally, a special thanks to Bing, Bob, and Dorothy.

Randy Mielke
February 1997

Introduction

The pairing of two complementary talents in the movies has been effectively utilized by Hollywood since filmmaking began. From Stan Laurel and Oliver Hardy to Mel Gibson and Danny Glover, the savvy give and take between two skillful actors has entertained audiences and piled up receipts at the box office. But no teaming has been so beneficial and endearing as the joining of Bob Hope and Bing Crosby in the seven "Road" pictures they made with Dorothy Lamour.

All the "Road" films followed the same basic format: a flimsy plot with adventurers Hope and Crosby caught in seemingly impossible situations. They would defeat the bad guys—usually utilizing the famous patty-cake routine—and vie with one another for Lamour's attention. A few ballads, duets, and comedy numbers were added for musical flavor. It all seemed to work.

In this day of mega-hit movies with millions of dollars being spent on productions and enormous returns being brought in at the box office, the "Road" films might seem out of their league. But for their time, they were financially successful films. In fact, all of the "Road" films, except the 1962 *The Road to Hong Kong* (the only one with a *"The"*), were among the top moneymakers in the year they were released, according to Cobbett Steinberg's *Film Facts*. Indeed, the trio did travel the "Road to Box Office."

Which leads to the road this book will cover—a fond look back on three screen stars, all with successful careers of their own, teamed together for journeys filled with miles of memories.

How They Met

One of the entertainment world's most famous and enduring friendships originated in 1932 on 48th Street in New York City. It happened near the renowned Friars Club, to which both a young comedian, Bob Hope, and a rising new singer, Bing Crosby, belonged. The two entertainers recognized each other on the street, exchanged a few pleasantries, and then went their separate ways. It was a rather low-key beginning for such a monumental partnership that spanned nearly 45 years.

But their paths were soon to cross again. Their talents, and the sincere affection they held for each other, would make them one of the most endearing teams in motion-picture history.

* * *

Part of Hope's career dilemma in the waning months of 1932 arose from his participation in a Broadway production called *Ballyhoo of 1932*, a show that was not faring too well. Even Hope's hilarious warm-up act could not salvage the weak musical. The critics were exceedingly nasty, and the show closed after just four months. Hope reluctantly returned to the vaudeville circuit, and his next job took him to New York's Capitol Theater in December of 1932.

Crosby was also touring New York in 1932, but on a much more positive note. He had left Paul Whiteman's band and then his own group, the Rhythm Boys, to pursue a solo singing career. His hit record "I Surrender Dear," a national show on CBS radio, and a good showing in his first major film, *The Big Broadcast of 1932*, had put him on the proverbial road to stardom. With his popularity on the rise, Crosby was scheduled to appear for a two-week engagement at the Capitol

1

Theater. It was his first personal appearance in New York since his success in the Paramount film. Hope was the master of ceremonies of the Capitol show.

As the emcee, Hope always received an advance list of the scheduled performers he would introduce each night. On one occasion, he was pleased to find Crosby's name heading the list. When Crosby arrived at the theater for the first show, Hope welcomed him warmly. Since meeting briefly several months before, the two had followed each other's show business careers with interest.

There are differing accounts as to how Hope and Crosby first started performing various comedy bits together. Some versions indicate that one or the other came to the theater early each day during the two-week run. It was decided that the two entertainers should try something different from the standard introductions Hope was using. Other versions imply that the two performers met and talked at a neighborhood bar during their engagement at the Capitol Theater. If they did happen to meet in a local bar during their run at the Capitol, it must have been at a speakeasy because Prohibition would not end for another year.

Regardless of where their discussions took place, the pair found that show business was only one of the things they had in common. People who saw the two entertainers together when they were not on stage during their engagement at the Capitol probably thought Hope and Crosby were just a couple of buddies trading old war stories. What these people were witnessing, in fact, was the birth of a classic partnership.

Hope and Crosby got along right from the start. They kidded each other repeatedly, but the verbal jousting was never done with any malice. The two men had genuine warmth and affection for each other, despite the often derogatory comments they made.

It was not long before the two entertainers realized they could transfer their competitive good humor to the Capitol stage. It was at this point that they began to develop some comedic ideas and came up with a few routines to replace Hope's usual semistraight introductions. Most of what they created was old-time vaudeville shtick, but it was funny and when it was performed, it seemed to delight the audiences. Their first routine featured Hope strolling confidently on stage alone.

"Ah, good evening, ladies and gents. I'm afraid we'll have to do without my partner tonight—some cad locked him in the washroom."

As the laughter died down, Crosby would saunter on from the

other side of the stage holding a brass doorknob attached to a piece of splintered wood.

"Good evening, ladies and gentlemen," Crosby said, as Hope looked on. "I feel I must apologize, you'll have to forgive me for working alone tonight—my partner has an upset stomach."

"Now wait a minute," Hope would retort in perfect timing. "I don't have an upset stomach."

"You will after you swallow this," Crosby would reply, waving the doorknob under Hope's nose.

Other comedy bits quickly followed, such as an impression of two orchestra leaders meeting on the street. Each performer pulled out a baton and led the other while he talked as if he were leading an orchestra. Next they performed an impression of two farmers meeting on the street. One of them asked in a down-home kind of drawl, "How are things down on the farm?" The other responded in like manner with: "It's pretty cold in the reading room." Then one "milked" the other's down-turned thumbs.

Even when the gags were not that funny, the appreciative audience laughed because it was apparent the two performers were having such a good time. From their first appearance at the Capitol Theater, Crosby and Hope went together like ham and eggs or Scotch and soda. By another lucky coincidence, Hope was signed by Paramount Pictures, and the two were able to renew their acquaintance around the studio lot.

After Hope's debut in feature films with *The Big Broadcast of 1938*, the gifted comedian was relegated to "B" picture status. On radio, however, he was becoming a big star because his spontaneous style and rapid-fire delivery delighted audiences. Hope often appeared on Crosby's radio show and Crosby on his.

The Hope-Crosby fictional feud that gained so much attention during this period was not something that had been planned. Their natural kidding of each other started to pervade the rehearsals of their radio shows when they appeared together. Their continual jesting drew almost unending laughter from bystanders and the crew. With such a good response from those on hand, the performers thought their ribbing and kidding might amuse a wider audience. They gradually worked their verbal jabs into the radio shows themselves. When the fabricated feud became popular with the public, the entertainers—and their writers—did nothing to derail it. Instead, they expanded it as much as possible.

It became customary for Hope to come to Crosby's *"Kraft Music Hall"* and for Crosby to show up at the *"Bob Hope Show"* armed with quips drafted by their writers. Hope kidded Crosby about his loud shirts and weird color combinations, his four sons, and his money. Crosby countered with cracks about Hope's cornball humor, his failed romances, his thrifty nature, and his slight paunch.

But neither celebrity was content to leave it at that. They developed a one-upsmanship approach with the help of their writers. The writers would say to Crosby, "When he calls you 'Fatty,' you say to him, 'That's not exactly baby fat you've got there yourself. I happen to know that Sophie Tucker lends you her cast-off girdles.'"

Then the writers would go to Hope, tell him what Crosby was going to say, and suggest, "Right ahead of his line you say, 'And don't pull that ancient wheeze about Sophie Tucker's girdle. There's no bounce left in that joke or the girdles.'" The technique fueled the feud and elated their fans.

It was this quick-witted banter that made the team work so well together. More often than not, neither performer was stopped in his tracks for a comeback or a put-down. Either by design—with the help of their writers—or by their own quick wit, each was ready with a clever line. There was rarely any dead time on air or on film. It worked to perfection.

* * *

While all this was going on, a young female singer who was a former Miss New Orleans beauty queen was making a name for herself in New York nightclubs. Her name was Dorothy Lamour.

Hope met Lamour while he was working in Broadway shows in the early 1930s. After a show, Hope would often take a midnight walk to unwind and get some exercise, and one of the places he stopped at was a night spot called One Fifth Avenue. The beautiful girl with the sultry voice who simply leaned against a wall and sang wonderfully was Lamour.

Hope saw Lamour again when she appeared at the Navarre Club on Central Park South, a favorite hangout for comedians, and the two became friends. Lamour would later appear with Hope in his first feature film, *The Big Broadcast of 1938*. In addition to the "Road" pictures that Hope and Lamour would do with Crosby, the comedian and sexy singer also appeared together in such films as *Caught in the Draft* (1941) and *My Favorite Brunette* (1947).

Crosby also met Lamour during those early days of her show business career, when she was singing with bandleader Herbie Kay. *Road to Singapore*, however, would be the first picture that the two singers would appear in together.

* * *

Several factors contributed to the rapport that Hope and Crosby so easily displayed on stage and in films.

Although both could toss insults with great accuracy, there was never any sting involved. The public accurately perceived that Bing Crosby and Bob Hope were two men who really liked each other. Crosby admired Hope's energy and ambition, and Hope revered Crosby's natural talent. They also shared a love of golf and other sports.

Another secret to the tandem's success was the different pace at which each of them worked. The old cliché of opposites attracting may have been the case with these two talented individuals. Crosby was easygoing and laid-back, whereas the impulsive Hope was always on the go. The combination seemed to work to both entertainers' satisfaction.

An example of how well Crosby and Hope worked together, and especially how at ease Crosby felt with Hope, was evidenced when actor Edward G. Robinson appeared on Crosby's radio show in the mid-thirties.

It was standard operating procedure at that time that Crosby's radio show did not include any ad-libs. Pleasurable as the show was, it had very little of the easygoing humor Crosby was capable of displaying. Everything was scripted, and each show was rehearsed and performed word for word with rarely any variation.

One day the show's producers arranged with guest star Edward G. Robinson to alter things just a bit, fully believing it would serve to loosen Crosby up. During one of their dialogues on the air, Robinson suddenly asked, "By the way, Bing, how's your golf score?"

Crosby was astounded. Thinking Robinson might have just skipped some pages, Crosby quickly flipped through his script but saw no lines about his golf score. He responded simply, "Oh, I'm getting down in the low eighties." He and Robinson continued the exchange, then returned to the script. Later in the show, Robinson again threw in an impromptu question, and Crosby answered it casually.

After the broadcast was over, however, Crosby was outraged. His producers tried to convince him that his engaging personality came across much better in the ad-lib situations, but Crosby was not one for surprises. He was not satisfied until his friends told him how natural the exchange with Robinson had seemed. After that, Crosby tolerated an occasional ad-lib. But from that incident, it is apparent that many of Crosby's ad-libs with Hope on radio, and later in films, were effective because he felt so at ease working with that particular comedian.

With numerous benefit appearances together and successful guest shots on each other's radio shows, it was only natural for Bing Crosby and Bob Hope to continue their acquaintance after Hope arrived at Paramount.

It was during this time that Crosby and actor Pat O'Brien began operating the Del Mar Race Track together. The pre-opening party for the racing season at the track turned out to be a classic evening of entertainment. Performers at the Del Mar Saturday night shindig included Crosby, O'Brien, Mary Martin, Jimmy Durante, Phil Harris, and Al Jolson—all displaying their talents for a select Hollywood crowd.

"Why don't you and I do some of those routines we did at the Capitol?" Crosby suggested to Hope.

"Sure thing," Hope said, never passing up an opportunity to perform.

Reportedly, it was at this affair that Crosby coined the nickname "Ski Nose" for Hope, and Hope in turn took it out on Crosby's unsuccessful race horses. Like many of the benefits they had performed over the years, the Del Mar show featured a number of vaudeville-like impressions and time-honored gags. They finished the show with a song, an old soft shoe, and a flourish.

The show-biz audience was in hysterics over the Hope-Crosby antics. One of those in attendance that night was William LeBaron, production chief at Paramount. When he returned to the studio, he told his aides what he had witnessed.

"Those two boys work well together," LeBaron said, not realizing that Hope and Crosby had started rehearsing together seven years before. "We ought to put them in a picture together."

Not a bad idea, as it turned out.

Taking Them
on the Road

In addition to William LeBaron, there were other Paramount bigwigs at the Del Mar Race Track that pivotal night in 1939 who thought Bob Hope and Bing Crosby made a good team. Harlan Thompson, who had enjoyed a great career on Broadway as a lyricist and librettist, was by this time a Paramount producer and was in the audience at Del Mar when Hope and Crosby performed their hilarious shtick. Thompson also reportedly perceived that Crosby and Hope had viable chemistry as a team. When he took his idea to the Paramount brass, however, he was turned down.

"No contrast," said one executive.

"Crosby needs a girl," said another, "and Hope needs a straight man. And Crosby isn't going to be a straight man for anybody."

"He's right," added a third. "You can't have a team without a straight man."

Thompson argued his case, but the answer was still no.

In 1939, Tinsel Town was going through a period of making South Sea island films which were designed to give the cinema-going public some relief from the harsh realities of life during the depression. As was often the case in Hollywood's heyday, company executives wanted to take advantage of the current vogue and get something into production and out to the public in short order.

Paramount owned a script called *The Road to Mandalay* which scriptwriters Frank Butler and Don Hartman had adapted from a South Sea tale entitled *Beach of Dreams* by Harry Hervey.

At first the studio wanted to cast affable Fred MacMurray and comedian Jack Oakie as two vagabond entertainers on the lam in the tropics. Both stars turned down the offer, however. Then the executives' thoughts turned to the combination of George Burns and Gracie Allen, maybe even with Crosby in the film, but Burns and Allen could not fit it into their schedule.

Still intrigued with the idea of teaming Hope and Crosby, Thompson reportedly discussed the concept with writers Butler and Hartman. They were working on *The Road to Mandalay* and had altered the concept from serious to funny. They had also changed the title. The new screenplay was called *Road to Singapore*. The name "Singapore" was used because the writers did not think "Mandalay" sounded treacherous enough. (Another reason for the change to "Singapore" was to avoid confusion with Al Jolson's hit song "Mandalay.") Butler and Hartman also were wise enough to include a part for a sexy film star.

Now everything started to make sense. Combine Bing Crosby and Bob Hope in one movie and add a girl. It all seemed like a winning combination: a foreign land, natives, music, a sexy starlet, Hope being a clown, and Crosby singing the ballads. The idea, first suggested lightly, became a hot business proposition, and Butler and Hartman continued to refine their script.

LeBaron, who also had been inspired by the comedic twosome at Del Mar, was reportedly the executive who sent for Dorothy Lamour. Lamour, a dark-haired beauty, had become a leading Paramount star as a result of her parts in the South Sea island pictures (such as John Ford's *The Hurricane* in 1937). LeBaron reasoned that Lamour and her sarong would supply the elements of glamour and sex the new partnership needed. She had already appeared with Hope in *The Big Broadcast of 1938*, but had not made a film with Crosby.

Lamour, however, remembered a different version of how the "Roads" came to be. She claims that one day after lunch in the Paramount commissary, she stopped at a table where Hope and Crosby were displaying their usual brand of hysterics. She left the commissary, still laughing, and bumped into two writer friends who asked her what she was laughing at. Lamour told them she had just been joking with Hope and Crosby and that if they could only come up with a story involving two crazy guys and a "gal in the middle," she would love to play her.

Soon after, the first "Road" story was turned into the front office and Lamour got her wish—Hope, Crosby, and she were set to star in it.

Whichever version is accurate, the fact remains that the *Road to Singapore* was on its way to being made.

Singapore did much to nurture the Hope-Crosby friendship. The two stars enjoyed each other's company and were often likened to two little boys who were just having fun at playtime.

The two celebrities often decorated their dressing rooms with retouched pictures of each other, adding and subtracting features here and there. Hope had Crosby's ears considerably enlarged for one shot, making a normally big pair of ears look like the handles on a loving-cup trophy. In another photo, Hope had a darkroom artist cross Crosby's eyes.

They also became offscreen chums. They shared a number of common interests, the principal one being golf, which they played every chance they got. This linkage furthered their friendly yet competitive nature that would come across on the screen.

As two performers who got along fabulously, Bob Hope and Bing Crosby also had fun with others during the production of their films. After they had made a few films together, they would often add things to the unedited versions to shake up the top brass. After doing some scenes together, for example, they would add little bits to amuse Buddy DeSylva, a production head at Paramount, because they knew he would be seeing the daily rushes. DeSylva had started to play a ukulele at one point, so Crosby and Hope would finish a scene, ask the director to keep the cameras rolling, and say, "Now let's try the same thing over again with a ukulele."

Few partners in show business history complemented each other so thoroughly. Hope was an outstanding gagster who could sing pretty well. Crosby was a supreme singer who was clever with a quip. In addition, Hope could handle the more physical comedy. As screen performers, neither dominated the other. They enhanced each other's strengths rather than overwhelming the other's weaknesses.

In many ways, Hope could be credited with being the glue that held everything together. A decent hoofer (that is how he started in show business), he also could carry a tune and was very good at harmonizing. On the other side of the coin, Hope radiated as a comedian, but Crosby and Lamour held their own with their light comedic touches.

In creating *Road to Singapore*, writers Butler and Hartman came up with a formula that was simple, yet surefire: Crosby is the debonair dreamer, Hope his trusting friend. Crosby is the romantic, promoting love songs to the exotic Lamour at every turn. Hope has an adolescent's ambitions regarding love, and although he appears at times to be close to his goal, he usually falls short of the mark.

Later, Hartman would describe a "Road" picture this way: "You take a piece of used chewing gum and flip it at a map. Wherever it sticks you can lay a 'Road' picture, so long as the people there are jokers who cook and eat strangers. If they're nasty and menacing, it'll be a good 'Road' picture. The key to the thing is menace offsetting humor."

Perhaps *Time* magazine summed it up best: "The road shows were rummage sales of stuff out of vaudeville, burlesque—marvelously shoddy masterpieces of farce and fantasy, stitched together with clichés and ad libs."

To describe the plot of a "Road" picture in one line: The boys are in a jam, or as many jams as possible, and they have to clown their way out.

It proved to be the beginning of a beautiful and successful partnership.

Road to Singapore, 1940

Whether anyone connected with the filming of *Road to Singapore* knew it or not, the stage was set for an abundance of frivolity and confusion. And no one came to know it quicker than Dorothy Lamour.

It was during the filming of *Road to Singapore* that Bob Hope and Bing Crosby started their hilarious ad-libbing that contributed immensely to the success of the "Roads." The two celebrities were already appearing on each other's radio shows, and their ingenious writers had developed an easygoing, semi-insulting rapport for them. Hope and Crosby carried this badgering, competitive spirit over into the filming of the *Road to Singapore*, and it all seemed very natural. Unfortunately, there were times when they got so carried away with their comedic tantrums that they completely forgot about Lamour.

Always the professional, Lamour was conscientious when it came to learning her lines before filming a scene. The night before she was to start filming *Road to Singapore*, Lamour reviewed the script of the film in which she was about to appear. When she arrived on the set the next morning, fully prepared to perform the scenes she had studied, director Victor Schertzinger was already shooting a scene with Crosby and Hope alone. As Lamour sat and watched, she slowly realized that nothing in their witty dialogue sounded even remotely familiar.

Lamour was then called to do her first scene, a three-shot with her standing between Hope and Crosby. As soon as the assistant director called "Action!" ad-libs between the two leads started flying everywhere. Lamour kept waiting for her cue and finally, in exasperation, blurted out, "Please, guys, when can I get my line in?" Hope and Crosby stopped dead, broke up laughing, and halted filming for ten minutes.

But the effortless banter between the two leads continued in subsequent takes, and Hope and Crosby kidded Lamour about it mercilessly. Fortunately, Lamour had a great sense of humor and took it all in stride. Later on in the filming, Crosby would yell, "If you find an opening, Dottie, just throw something in."

Yet the finished product is not as disorganized as it would seem. There are frivolity and ad-libs, to be sure, but the overall effect is one of smoothly moving comedy and realistic situations. The end result is a credit to the professionalism of all three performers.

The somewhat unusual antics perpetrated by the two leads, however, were not surefire, not even in their own minds. Curious about the reactions of the stuffy front office to their childlike mischief, Hope and Crosby would occasionally sneak up to the projection room where the studio executives were watching the daily rushes. Most of the big honchos were present, and spirited laughter could be heard from outside the door. The crooner and the comic knew they were in.

Lamour decided it was a waste of time to learn her lines in the script. She decided to briefly read over the next day's work to get an idea of what was happening, but she did not memorize her lines as she had before. Instead, she got a good night's sleep to be in shape for the next morning's ad-libs by the frolicking Hope and Crosby.

Schertzinger, a patient director, seemed content to put up with all the nonsense happening around him. He would voice a mild objection here and there, but for the most part, he let the leads have their fun. Perhaps he intuitively knew their antics and merriment would pay off in the end and that the result would seem spontaneous.

Schertzinger helped set the musical and comedic tone for the entire series. In addition to directing *Road to Singapore*, he also directed the team's second film, *Road to Zanzibar*.

Schertzinger was a congenial man and a gifted violinist and songwriter. (He played with the John Philip Sousa band and was a concert violinist in Europe for several years.) But aside from his musical talent, he had directed some fine pictures for RKO, Fox, and Columbia and was even nominated for a Best Director Academy Award in 1934 for his *One Night of Love*. He lost to Frank Capra for the latter's direction of *It Happened One Night*. The only drawback in Schertzinger's directing of the first "Road" picture was that he had little experience with comedy. Since *Singapore* originally was envisioned more as a musical than a comedic picture, Paramount had signed Schertzinger to direct it because of his musical background.

Schertzinger was a quiet, laid-back individual who directed his pictures in a leisurely fashion. When Crosby and Hope tore haphazardly into a scene, ad-libbing at will, Schertzinger grabbed a script and searched desperately for the lines they were saying. When he couldn't find them, he had every intention of halting them midsentence and asking them to do the scene the way it was written. However, noticing that the rest of the cast and the entire crew were laughing at their antics, Schertzinger realized that the kind of movie being filmed each day was spontaneous and highly entertaining. He allowed the duo to ramble on.

Schertzinger's personality and poise were well suited for the Hope-Crosby technique, and he was able to adjust to their freewheeling style, as the filming of a scene in *Singapore* illustrates.

In those days, most directors would film a master shot taking in the whole scene, then move in closer for a medium shot, then shoot each principal actor in close-ups. Later the scene would be cut and edited together with the various angles intertwined.

In *Singapore*, the three principals acted out a scene which lasted about five minutes. In the scene, Crosby and Hope typically threw lines back and forth while a bewildered Lamour tried to get a word in whenever she could.

"Cut and print!" said Schertzinger at the end of the scene. "Let's go to the next set-up."

A bit surprised, the assistant director drew Schertzinger aside and asked him if he had noticed that Hope had stepped out of the light of the scene. Schertzinger acknowledged that he was aware of it.

"But don't you want to make another shot," asked the assistant director, "or get some other angles for protection?"

"No," Schertzinger said, reverting to his musical background for an explanation. "That scene was like a piece of music; it was well orchestrated and it flowed beautifully. Maybe the flutes were off key or the cellos didn't come in at the right time. But the total performance was great. I could shoot that scene again, but the actors would not have the same spark they had the first time. And if I made a lot of protection shots, the producers would find some way to foul up the scene in the cutting room. Next set-up!"

In many ways, Schertzinger was an ideal director for the "Road" films. He reportedly said at one point during the filming: "You know, I really shouldn't take any money for this job. All I do is say 'stop' and 'go.'"

Paramount had chosen Schertzinger to direct the picture because of his musical background. In addition to his directing, Schertzinger even contributed the music for two songs in the film.

But the backbone of the music in *Road to Singapore* and later "Road" films was Johnny Burke.

Burke started out as a composer and began writing songs in the late 1920s. By 1930 he had created the music for the successful *Yours and Mine*, with George Little providing the lyrics. Burke made a trip to glitzy Hollywood that same year to write the music for George Little's words in a Fox musical called *Let's Go Places*.

Between that Hollywood trip and 1936 when he permanently settled down on the West Coast, Burke did some successful writing with Harold Spina. But for this collaboration, he switched from composing the music to writing the lyrics. After that, Burke, with Arthur Johnston, wrote "Annie Doesn't Live Here Anymore" for Crosby, which led to Crosby giving the pair an opportunity to write the score for the 1936 film *Pennies from Heaven*. From that time on, Burke became Crosby's nearly exclusive lyric writer for films.

Shortly after *Pennies from Heaven*, Burke teamed up with composer James V. Monaco. For *Road to Singapore*, which was made in 1940, Monaco supplied the music for three songs—"Too Romantic," "Sweet Potato Piper," and "Kaigoon"—while Burke penned the lyrics. Burke and Monaco's moving "Too Romantic" for Crosby and Lamour is a perfect ballad for Crosby's style. "Sweet Potato Piper," a bright and lively tune performed by the three leads, delighted audiences.

In addition, director Victor Schertzinger wrote the music for two more songs to which Burke added the lyrics. Burke teamed with Schertzinger for Lamour's "The Moon and the Willow Tree" and the energetic "Captain Custard" for Hope and Crosby.

The "Road" series concentrated more on comedy in subsequent films and never fully regained the musical aspect until *Road to Rio* in 1947.

But *Road to Singapore* was not without its comedic moments. Based on a story by Harry Hervey, the screenplay written by Frank Butler and Don Hartman was heavily infused with comedy bits and gags.

Although Bing Crosby and Bob Hope appeared to make their nutty, humorous comments off the cuff in the "Road" films (and, indeed, sometimes they did), most of the ad-libbing in the pictures was generated by the screenwriters or, in more cases than not, the two stars' gag writers. The easygoing and quick-witted banter between the two leads was an appealing facet which contributed greatly to the series' success.

The simple yet refreshing system came about merely as a result of Hope and Crosby performing on each other's radio shows where their writers had developed a semi-insulting conflict between the two entertainers. Crosby once said that the writers found it easier to write disparaging jokes for them to trade than any other kind of humor. The verbal sparring carried over into their moviemaking and enabled the "Road" pictures to have an air of excitement usually found only in connection with live entertainment.

Although Bob Hope and Bing Crosby insisted that they often created the humorous lines, they did employ gag writer Barney Dean to augment the ad-libs and comedy in the early pictures. Dean was an ex-vaudeville knockabout comedian who, from his bare feet to his bald head, stood just over five feet tall.

"Gags can't be played against gags," said Crosby at the time. "They have to be played against something more serious, even though the serious stuff is melodramatic. Hope and I invent many of these gag escapes from predicaments as we go along, and to prevent our imagination from flagging, we prevailed upon Paramount to employ Barney Dean, whom we remembered from our vaudeville days."

According to Hope, the gnomelike Dean was frequently unemployed and therefore available. When Hope and Crosby were making *Road to Singapore*, Dean strolled onto the set selling Christmas cards, but soon it was he who was dishing out the gifts in the form of gags. Hope suggested that Dean stay on the set while they were shooting the film to see if he could come up with some amusing bits. Hope theorized that even if the two stars did not use the comedy material, it might serve as a springboard for another gag.

Dean went to work immediately, and although he never really wrote anything, the diminutive gag writer stayed on the set at all times, intently watching rehearsals. Before a scene, Dean might take Crosby or Hope aside and say: "Wouldn't it be funnier if you said this?" and more often than not, he would come up with some funny bit or ingenious piece of dialogue. He also would suggest a different bit of business here or an odd gesture there, and it usually wound up as a big laugh in the finished film.

Mel Frank, who cowrote *Road to Utopia* and *The Road to Hong Kong* with Norman Panama, said almost every comedic exchange in the films was scripted. "To my knowledge, there was not one single ad-lib that was not written for them. Mind you, they may have called us in and said we need a little something ... but I can show you the scripts that we [Panama and Frank] were involved in—and it was all on paper."

In later years Hope admitted that he used gag writers on occasion. "As my movie career started to develop momentum, I developed a mode of operation which has continued through the years. Whenever I received a movie script, I handed it to my gag writers. They submitted jokes to punch up scenes in the picture."

There is no reason to believe that this type of comedic enhancement was not utilized on the "Road" pictures also. But the freewheeling style of the two entertainers originally brought shouts of disdain from the writers of the "Road" pictures.

Frank Butler and Don Hartman, who wrote *Road to Singapore* as well as *Road to Zanzibar* and *Road to Morocco*, resented Crosby and Hope's tampering with their original scripts. During the filming of *Singapore*, one of the writers reportedly came on the set and issued a complaint, which only gave the two stars more opportunity to needle him. "If you hear anything that sounds like one of your lines," said Hope, "just yell 'Bingo!'"

The plot of *Road to Singapore* was typical of many prewar comedies of the time. Josh Mallon (Crosby), the son of shipping magnate Charles Coburn, is fed up with the stuffy life and his snobbish fiancée (Judith Barrett), so he ships out to the South Pacific with a low-brow friend, Ace Lannigan (Hope). They land on the mythical isle of Kaigoon on their way to Singapore. (They never make it to Singapore, and such is their fate in the ensuing films: they rarely make it to the end of the road.)

On Kaigoon, they rescue a native entertainer, Mima (Lamour), from the cruel Caesar (Anthony Quinn). After a series of adventures, Crosby is claimed by his father and fiancée and Hope leaves with Lamour. Crosby has second thoughts, and he escapes after hearing that Hope and Lamour are in the vicinity, leaving his fiancée in the lurch. It turns out that Hope hasn't married Lamour. "You're the dopey-looking kluck she wants," Hope tells Crosby.

For the most part, critics were kind, and *Road to Singapore* received generally favorable reviews. *Motion Picture Herald* stated, "Two of the most congenially harmonized performances caught by the camera in recent years." *Picture Show* thought the film was "a deft blend of romance and comedy, songs and fisticuffs." *Variety* noted that "Much of the humor is wacky and nonsensical, but made palatable in the manner of presentation by the Crosby-Hope team." Frank S. Nugent of the *New York Times* observed, however, "The comedy is going along swimmingly until boys meet sarong."

As would be the case in future "Roads," *Road to Singapore* exhibited some talented performers in supporting roles. In several cases throughout the "Road" series, the supporting characters elevated the films to a slightly higher level.

Right from the start, the "Road" series had a strong supporting player in Anthony Quinn. Although relatively unknown in 1940, Quinn went on to become a star in his own right with films such as *Lust for Life* (1956), *Lawrence of Arabia* (1962), *Requiem for a Heavyweight* (1962), and *Zorba the Greek* (1963).

In *Road to Singapore*, Quinn appeared as Caesar, the whip-snapping, possessive dancing partner of Dorothy Lamour. He would appear in the "Road" series again in *Road to Morocco*, playing Mullay Kasim, the desert prince who plans to marry Lamour.

In many ways Quinn was the perfect foil for Hope and Crosby. Big and menacing—and in *Road to Singapore* a man of few words—he epitomized the strong, silent types of that era.

Quinn's presence also gave Crosby and Hope more fuel for their verbal feud. In one altercation scene, Crosby was supposed to take a swipe at Quinn. Although he was not really supposed to hit him, Crosby somehow mistimed the blow and hit Quinn squarely in the jaw. Instead of Quinn reacting or going down, he just stood there. That prompted Hope to say: "You can't hit very hard, can you, Bing?"

Ironically, at the time of Quinn's appearance in *Road to Singapore*, he was earning extra money entertaining at parties, charging two dollars a night doing imitations of Bing Crosby, Louis Armstrong, and Maurice Chevalier.

Anthony Quinn won the Oscar for Best Supporting Actor in *Viva Zapata* (1952) and also for *Lust for Life* and was nominated for Best Actor in *Wild is the Wind* (1957) and *Zorba the Greek*. He also appeared in the war epic *Back to Bataan* (1945) and the action/adventure movie *The Guns of Navarone* (1961).

Another talented actor who appeared in *Road to Singapore* was Charles Coburn. Coburn almost always played cigar-chomping, monocled fatherly types and the same was true in *Road to Singapore*, in which he portrayed Crosby's impatient and wealthy father.

Coburn also played father to some other big stars. He was Jimmy Stewart's dad in *Vivacious Lady* (1938), Cary Grant's father in *In Name*

Only (1939), and the cardsharper daddy of Barbara Stanwyck in *The Lady Eve* (1941).

Coburn was a master of character parts. His distinctive, somewhat flabby face could register hate, amusement, or tenderness with great ease. The contrast is apparent from his portrayal of a comedic character in *Road to Singapore* in 1940 and his convincingly sadistic Dr. Henry Gordon in *King's Row* only a year later.

By convincing Jean Arthur to share her apartment with him in war-crowded Washington in *The More the Merrier* (1943), Coburn won a Best Supporting Actor Academy Award. He was nominated for Best Supporting Actor for *The Devil and Miss Jones* in 1941, also with Arthur, and then was nominated again for the grandfather role of Alexander "Dandy" Gow in *The Green Years* (1946).

Coburn's other movies include *Bachelor Mother* (1939), *The Story of Alexander Graham Bell* (1939), *In This Our Life* (1942), *Monkey Business* (1952) with Cary Grant and Ginger Rogers, and *Gentlemen Prefer Blondes* (1953).

In *Road to Singapore*, walrus-mustachioed comedian Jerry Colonna made the first of three appearances in the "Road" series. (He also appeared in cameo roles in *Rio* and *Hong Kong*.) In *Singapore*, Colonna shines in a funny bit about Hope ruining Colonna's white suit with spot remover. In the scene, Hope, Crosby, and Lamour are trying to scrape together some money by marketing a miracle spot remover to the local natives. Colonna ambles by, is overpowered by the threesome, and is subjected to a spot remover demonstration, only to have the spot remover create soap suds that expand out of control and leave nothing left of his coat lapel.

Colonna was best known for his bizarre, professor-type image on Hope's radio shows and was a perennial favorite on Hope's United Services Organization (USO) Christmas shows overseas. Other films in which Colonna appeared include *52nd Street* and *Rosalie*, both in 1937. *The Road to Hong Kong* was his last film appearance.

Road to Singapore is a funny musical film with a better constructed plot than some of the later "Roads." But in this first "Road" film, the two leading characters are not fully developed. Crosby, as the wealthy shipping heir, plays his role conservatively and is a bit rigid. Hope, the easygoing wanderer, is more the perpetrator of the outrageous schemes. In later films, Crosby is the one behind the scams, while Hope plays the victim.

But the basic inspirations that would propel the series are there:

Hope and Crosby bat witty lines back and forth, combine their talents in rollicking musical numbers, and introduce the running gag of patty-caking prior to the start of a melee.

The predictable, yet humorous patty-cake routine became a staple in almost all future "Road" pictures. Whenever a menacing figure threatens the boys, they stop, bend their knees, and, with insipid expressions on their faces, start playing patty-cake. The villain is usually so dumfounded that he stops to watch them, whereupon they flatten him and run.

The theme of anti-establishment appears in *Singapore* and again in the later "Roads." The two men are always ducking authorities because of unkept promises to local women or outrageous plans to swindle the native population.

Much of the appeal of *Singapore*, as well as of later "Road" films, lies in the camaraderie between Bob Hope and Bing Crosby. Although they appear to be buddies, they actually engage in rivalry over money, sex, and personal vanity. In the "Road" films, both men share an aversion to matrimony and a distaste for physical violence. In *Singapore* and ensuing films, they display an ability to wisecrack their way out of tight spots using old vaudeville routines.

As appealing as *Road to Singapore* is, it is considered by some to contain a few flaws. Mainly, the film comes off as a bit uneven. When Crosby loses Lamour to Hope, for example, the scene appears overly maudlin. The three are in their grass-thatched, wooden hut and the boys ask Lamour to choose between them. Lamour goes the noble route (knowing that Crosby has a fiancée) and picks Hope. Instead of Crosby being impertinent (as would be the case in later films), he is philosophical when he tells Lamour: "He'll cause you a lot of trouble and never make a quarter, but he can hand you a million laughs."

The exotic element of *Singapore*, however, was perfect for the early war years. What better way to keep America's mind off the realities of life than watching two guys frolic on a South Sea island?

In one scene, Crosby, Hope, and Lamour perform a modest musical number in the midst of a small village filled with bewildered natives watching the trio. On a makeshift stage, the three perform the mellifluous melodies of "Sweet Potato Piper" with Crosby singing the song, Lamour playing guitar, and Hope on an ocarina, a gourdlike instrument the shape and size of a sweet potato. As Hope and Lamour play, Crosby goes into a soft-shoe dance until it is Hope's turn to kick up his heels while Crosby toots on a sweet potato pipe. Then

Mima (Dorothy Lamour) tends to tidying up the place as Josh Mallon (Bing Crosby) and Ace Lannigan (Bob Hope) look on in *Road to Singapore* (1940).

Hope and Crosby play their instruments together, and finally Lamour joins in and the three make rudimentary harmonies on the musical gadgets: Lamour plays the largest ocarina, Crosby the smallest, Hope the medium-sized sweet potato. The tune and the setting of the scene permitted considerable freedom of grimaces and gestures. Needless to say, all three took full advantage of that latitude.

In the film, Lamour moves in with the boys in their two-room domicile as their housekeeper. The idea was a little racy for 1940, but the censors made sure that everything in the little cottage was on the up-and-up. In one of the funniest scenes, the boys, broke and hungry, devise a way to gather some food. Crosby takes a concoction of baking flour and clay brick shavings that Hope was planning to sell to the natives as cockroach killer and uses the mixture to darken their skin. Then the trio fashions towel-like attire for the boys from the curtains Lamour has installed in the hut. The next scene features Hope and Crosby with darkened skin, cloth turbans and striped wraparound garments with only their shoulders exposed, sitting at a native wedding feast.

Character actress Elvia Allman surprises Ace Lannigan (Bob Hope) and Josh Mallon (Bing Crosby) in the song "Captain Custard" from the film *Road to Singapore* (1940).

As would be the case during the filming of future "Road" films, the offscreen antics of the three leads were plentiful. When Schertzinger took particular trouble with a close-up shot of Crosby's face, Hope interfered.

"You're not worried about anybody knowing what he looks like, are you?" Hope questioned seriously. "We're trying to keep that from the country—until they get penicillin around to everybody."

"Come, dad," Crosby chided Hope, "don't be jealous. We'll do your puss full justice when we get those stronger lenses."

As much as Hope and Crosby kidded Lamour about tossing in an errant line here and there, she learned to compete with the two when it came to offscreen levity.

In one scene in *Singapore*, Lamour is washing the table with a washcloth and water from an old-fashioned wooden bucket. Since regular soapsuds would have melted under the hot lights, the special effects department designed fake suds that had a more durable consistency.

During a lunch break, Hope began throwing soapsuds at Crosby and Lamour. Then Crosby got into it, and they both began throwing them at Lamour. As they ran across the soundstage, Lamour grabbed a huge can of the special suds and ran after them. In the commissary, which was filled with lunch-goers at the time, she caught them and dumped the whole can over their heads. The spontaneous free-for-all provided plenty of amusement for the other actors and executives who were having lunch, but Schertzinger was not too thrilled. It meant that the trio's hair, along with all their clothes, had to be dried and their makeup reapplied. That all took time, and time was money to the studio. Yet it was this unexpected merriment—almost like a circus atmosphere—that prompted hairdressers, cameramen, and other crew members to vie for assignments to this and subsequent "Road" pictures.

The appeal of these films did not stop with the cast and crew. Movie audiences also liked them. Approximately four months after the shooting started, *Road to Singapore* premiered in New York, and the public flocked to it. This was something new; this was the tonic the troubled world needed.

And it was only the beginning.

Road to Singapore
A Paramount Picture

Released: March 1940
Running time: 84 minutes

Producer Harlan Thompson; *Assistant to the Producer* C. Mick; *Production Secretary* Mary Barnsley; *Director* Victor Schertzinger; *1st Assistant Director* George Templeton; *2d Assistant Director* Alvin Ganzer; *Directorial Secretary* Eleanore Edwards; *Screenplay* Don Hartman and Frank Butler; *Based on a story by* Harry Hervey; *Director of Photography* William C. Mellor; *Second Cameraman* Neal Beckner; *Art Direction* Hans Dreier and Robert Odell; *Film Editor* Paul Weatherwax; *Transparency Projection Shots* Farciot Edouart (assisted by Wallace Kelley and Loyal Griggs); *Costumes* Edith Head. *Musical Director* Victor Young; *Scoring Conductor and Musical Preparation* I. Talbot; *Orchestration* L. Shuken, C. Bradshaw; *Vocal Director* C. Henderson; *Pianist* Ray Turner; *Sound Recording by* Earl Hayman and John Cope; *Dance Director* LeRoy Prinz; *Assistant Dance Directors* Edward Prinz, Paula DeCardo; *Dance Secretary* Margaret McCarthy; *Unit Manager* H. Schwartz; *Supervisory Set Dresser* A. E. Freudeman; *Hairdressing Supervisor* Leonora Sabine; *Makeup Supervisor* Wally Westmore.
Songs: "Too Romantic," "Sweet Potato Piper," and "Kaigoon." Lyrics by Johnny Burke. Music by James V. Monaco. "The Moon and the

Willow Tree" and "Captain Custard." Lyrics by Johnny Burke. Music by Victor Schertzinger.

CAST

Josh Mallon	Bing Crosby
Mima	Dorothy Lamour
Ace Lannigan	Bob Hope
Joshua Mallon IV	Charles Coburn
Gloria Wycott	Judith Barrett
Caesar	Anthony Quinn
Achilles Bombanassa	Jerry Colonna
Timothy Willow	Johnny Arthur
Morgan Wycott	Pierre Watkin
Gordon Wycott	Gaylord Pendleton
Sir Malcolm Drake	Miles Mander
Zato	Pedro Regas
Babe	Greta Granstedt
Bill	Edward Gargan
Fred	Don Brodie
Sailor	John Kelly
Sailor's Wife	Kitty Kelly
Father	Roger Gray
Secretary	Harry C. Bradley
Cameraman	Richard Keene
Columnist	Jack Pepper
Native Shopkeeper	Belle Mitchell
Native Boy	Benny Inocencio
Ninky Poo	Gloria Franklin
1st Native Policeman	Fred Malatesta
2d Native Policeman	Bob St. Angelo
Native Dancing Girl	Carmen D'Antonio
High Priest	Monte Blue
Native Immigration Officer	Robert O'Connor
Ship's Officer	Cyril Ring
Boy	Larry Harris
Boy	Payne Johnson
Boy	Freddie Walburn
Proprietress	Marguerita Padula
Chaperon	Grace Hayle
Society Girl	Helen Lynd
Ship's Officer	Richard Tucker
Homely Girl	Elvia Allman
Bartender	Arthur Q. Bryan
Man	Jack Chapin
Dumb Looking Little Guy	Bobby Barber
Native Dancing Girl	Paula DeCardo

Road to Zanzibar, 1941

As sequel crazy as film studios would become in the latter portion of the twentieth century, they were no different in the 1940s. As soon as Paramount realized *Road to Singapore* was a bona fide hit, it started lining up the next "Road" picture.

The "Road" series, however, was not originally envisioned as a series at all. It more or less became a series when a writer named Sy Bartlett wrote a story called *Find Colonel Fawcett* that was about two guys who were journeying through the menacing Madagascar jungles.

The main problem with Bartlett's script, however, was its similarity to a recently released movie titled *Stanley and Livingston*. Since both scripts were highly dramatic, Don Hartman took Bartlett's *Fawcett* script, gagged it up a bit, and renamed it *Road to Zanzibar*. Hartman and Frank Butler, the writers of *Road to Singapore*, then finalized the *Zanzibar* screenplay and created the second "Road" for the intrepid adventurers.

Paramount wisely stuck very close to the winning formula that worked in *Road to Singapore* in terms of production staff. In addition to Hartman and Butler, the studio kept the same director, Victor Schertzinger.

For *Road to Zanzibar*, Schertzinger applied what he had learned about the Hope-Crosby chemistry from the first escapade and helped to establish the duo's characters for the rest of the "Roads." Schertzinger thought Crosby was at his funniest as the schemer and Hope much more humorous as the victim. The scenes seemed to flow better when Crosby played the lover who succeeds and Hope portrayed the apprehensive dupe.

In *Road to Zanzibar*, all of the "Road" elements of the later pictures started to merge. The picture opens with carnival huckster Chuck Reardon (Crosby), complete with straw hat and bamboo cane, singing "You Lucky People, You" to a gathering of citizens at a small carnival in deep, dark Africa. Outside the carnival tent, Crosby is shamelessly touting an attraction called Fearless Frazier (Hope), the Living Bullet. Meanwhile, inside the shelter, Hope is ready to be stuffed into the muzzle of an oversized cannon. Despite his gala appearance of skintight jump suit accented with spangles on his shorts, collar, and wrists and a white helmet with a skull and crossbones emblazoned on it, he is not thrilled with the situation. "I don't mind being drafted," Hope complains, "but not for ammunition."

Hope then asks their blonde assistant, "Where were you last night?"

"With my grandmother," she replies.

"Yeah? Well your grandmother got into bed with me at 4 o'clock this morning and he had lip rouge all over his face."

Crosby channels the reluctant crowd into the carnival tent, and they watch the launching of an unknown projectile from the cannon. In reality, a dummy is shot from the cannon, and it hits a circus tent and begins a fire that destroys the entire carnival. Realizing what has happened, the owner and his associates set off in pursuit of Hope and Crosby, and the flight begins.

The necessary ingredients for the "Road" they are about to travel are established in the first few minutes of the film: Crosby is the schemer, Hope is the victim; Crosby the lover, Hope the loser. Both are involved in some form of deceit or betrayal which makes it imperative that they stay on the lam for most of the picture. (In *Zanzibar*, Crosby's character is always devising some wild money-making scheme, while Hope wants only to get back home.)

This sense of mobility is part of what made all the "Roads" work. Bing Crosby and Bob Hope are never in one place long enough for boredom to set in. As soon as one locale is depleted of all its comedic possibilities, the script writers send the travelers on their way.

Their flights on the byways inevitably lead to some opportunity to perform a song, a dance, or a comedy routine. In *Zanzibar*, for example, they are escaping police and are cornered in a nightclub, so they try to exit by going on stage. Crosby, in a suit and bow tie, and Hope, in a light-colored suit with dark shirt, jump up on stage with about 12 chorus girls who are adorned in skimpy costumes, capes, hats, and feathers. The adventurers are in the midst of a chorus kick line and try to partake in the dance routine. The audience responds favorably to their awkward attempts to be part of the dance. Eventually the girls leave the stage, and a scenery backdrop comes down as Hope and Crosby take their bows. The two then grab batons and pretend to be orchestra leaders meeting on the boulevard. They conduct each other's conversations and wind up dueling with the batons, completing an old vaudeville routine the two had acted out countless times before.

After their brush with the law, an eccentric gentleman (Eric Blore) takes a liking to the boys and pays for the carnival damage in order to keep them out of jail. Crosby then spends the money that he and Hope have saved on a phony diamond mine he purchases from Blore. Hope manages to get the money back, only to be conned by Una Merkel into saving Dorothy Lamour from "white slavery." As Merkel and Lamour have done several times before, they work out a deal with the slave auctioneer (Douglass Dumbrille), who splits the money with them. The two stranded girls persuade the vulnerable boys to take them on a long safari to meet Lamour's intended beau. On the safari, both Hope and Crosby fall in love with Lamour.

Road to Zanzibar proved to be an even bigger box-office hit than the first "Road" picture, and a majority of the critics liked it, too. "Mostly nonsense, but it is nonsense of the most delightful sort," proclaimed Howard Barnes of the *New York Herald Tribune. Variety*, however, saw it a little differently: "[*Zanzibar*] lacks the compactness and spontaneity of its predecessor."

For *Road to Zanzibar*, the traveling trio again was blessed with competent supporting personnel. Una Merkel played Julia Quimby, Lamour's pal, in *Zanzibar* and also was a friend to heroine Eleanor Powell in *Born to Dance* (1936). The blonde-haired and blue-eyed Merkel often played the "girl with the wisecracks" and did so in *Zanzibar*. She also is known for her part in the hair-pulling fight with Marlene Dietrich in *Destry Rides Again* (1939).

But Merkel gained greater fame later in her film career. She was nominated for a Best Supporting Actress Academy Award as Geraldine Page's embittered mother in *Summer and Smoke* (1961). Other films Merkel appeared in include *42nd Street* (1933), W. C. Fields' *The Bank Dick* (1940), Burt Lancaster's *The Kentuckian* (1955), and *The Parent Trap* (1961).

Character actor Eric Blore played Charles Kimble of Kimble Diamond Mines in *Road to Zanzibar*. Kimble is an eccentric who delights in selling worthless mines to unsuspecting people. Blore was used to portraying quirky characters but usually was cast as the hired help, as evidenced by his string of movies with Fred Astaire and Ginger Rogers.

Blore played a waiter in *The Gay Divorcee* (1934); Bates, the man-servant in *Top Hat* (1935); Gordon, the huffy dance-school manager in *Swing Time* (1936); and Cecil Flintridge, the hotel floor manager in *Shall We Dance* (1937). Blore also appeared in *The Lady Eve* and *Sullivan's Travels*, both in 1941. In the 1940s, Blore assumed the role of Jamison, the bumptious butler/man Friday supporting Warren Williams in *The Lone Wolf* detective series.

Veteran character actor Douglass Dumbrille had a small part as a slave trader in *Zanzibar*, but would appear again in a larger role in *Road to Utopia*. Other performers in the cast of *Road to Zanzibar* included Luis Alberni, Joan Marsh, Ethel Greer, Iris Adrian, and Georges Renavent.

Although geared more for comedy than its predecessor, *Zanzibar* offered its share of nice musical moments. But for this "Road," Johnny Burke had a new songwriting partner.

For years, many people in the music business said Crosby's ideal type of song featured singsong accents, presenting a rhythm perfectly tailored to Crosby's pleasant vocal manner. Many musical folk felt Jimmy Van Heusen to be the perfect composer for the Crosby style. James V. Monaco, who had been writing music to accompany Johnny Burke's words for the last four years, was getting tired and did not feel well. There also was speculation that he and Burke had trouble getting along. Whatever the circumstances, a replacement composer was needed and Jimmy Van Heusen became the logical choice.

Van Heusen was born Edward Chester Babcock (a name that Hope would "borrow" for his character in *The Road to Hong Kong*) and began composing songs in high school. After landing a job with a local radio station as a part-time announcer and then as a pianist and singer, he sometimes worked his own compositions into his programs. During that time, at the station manager's urging, he changed his name to James Van Heusen, taking his last name from a popular brand of shirts he had seen advertised.

In typical manner for young songwriters, Van Heusen knocked around composing songs and spending time as a staff pianist for several New York music publishing houses. Burke met Van Heusen on a trip to New York in the mid–1930s.

In 1939, Van Heusen and lyricist Edward de Lange wrote the

songs for a swing version of Shakespeare's *A Midsummer Night's Dream*, titled *Swingin' the Dream*. The show flopped on Broadway, but one of its songs, "Darn That Dream," became a pop hit. By 1940, Van Heusen songs were catching on, and one, "Imagination," teamed him with Burke who was by this time a Hollywood veteran. That same year Burke and Van Heusen wrote the songs for *Love Thy Neighbor*, a Paramount musical teaming radio "feuders" Jack Benny and Fred Allen.

At Paramount, Van Heusen and Burke were assigned, at Crosby's request, to *Road to Zanzibar*.

In *Zanzibar*, Burke and Van Heusen worked the partnership well with the Crosby ballad "It's Always You" and the lighthearted "You Lucky People, You," also sung by Crosby. Other songs included Lamour's "You're Dangerous," "African Etude," "Birds of a Feather," and the title theme.

As good as the music was, *Road to Zanzibar* is still very much a comedy. It is in *Zanzibar* that some of the best one-upmanship of Hope and Crosby concerning women is displayed. In a memorable scene on the safari, Hope and Crosby are in their tent while Hope prepares for a date with Lamour. Both are clad in khaki-colored safari outfits complete with pith helmets. Hope is combing his hair and adding some talcum powder down the front of his shirt as Crosby starts to mix a "malaria preventive" while trying to convince Hope he's coming down with the malady. Hope resists at first, but then succumbs to Crosby's subtle persuasiveness and drinks the medicine, which turns out to be a sedative. Crosby then assumes Hope's place on the date with Lamour while Hope is forced to sleep off the sedative. On numerous occasions in the film, each tries to convince the other that Lamour really wants him, not the other guy. It is inspired comedy dialogue that appeared again in other films, but the prototype was established in *Zanzibar*.

An example of the style is typified by Hope sitting on a cot in his tent making a beaded necklace as a present for Lamour while Crosby looks on.

> Hope: "It's a token of my steam."
> Crosby: "Esteem is the word."
> Hope: "No, no, steam. I was hot that night."

In addition to the clever dialogue regarding women and relationships, *Zanzibar* was the first Hope-Crosby "Road" film to start biting the hand that fed them by poking fun at the movie industry. At an early point in the film, the two travelers are in a hotel room when they are

Una Merkel, Bing Crosby, Bob Hope, and Dorothy Lamour rest between scenes on the set of *Road to Zanzibar* **(1941).**

visited by the man to whom Hope tried to sell the fake diamond mine. The man has brought with him a personal enforcer who stands a full head taller than Hope or Crosby. As the boys try the patty-cake routine on the thug, he bops them on the head and two stars sprawl to the floor. As Hope recovers his composure, he says: "He must have seen the picture," referring to the same bit they executed successfully in *Road to Singapore*. (The patty-cake routine does work later in the picture, however, when they use it on natives who think it is a joke and start joyously belting each other.)

Although most of the "Road" films had inside jokes and references to the movie industry, *Zanzibar* was the first to start the ball rolling fast and feverishly in that direction. In a takeoff on romantic songs, Crosby sings "It's Always You" while he and Lamour are in a canoe floating down a deserted river in the middle of a densely wooded jungle. The two vocalists comment on how background music in movies seems to come out of nowhere and immediately rake their hands across the water to procure the sound of a harp while a dulcet bird aids Crosby in setting his pitch.

As had been the case with *Singapore*, ad-libbing became a common occurrence on the set of *Zanzibar*, with each of the leads trying to top the other with comebacks and one-liners. All of this disturbed the originators Butler and Hartman, who fought against changing anything they had written.

"They weren't really happy until they saw the results at the box office," said Hope. "They thought we were messing their scripts up, but after the box office results came in, they were very happy to be associated, like everybody else!"

An example of the "inspired" dialogue came during the filming of a safari scene that was intended to be silent. Although there was not supposed to be any dialogue between the leads, microphones were set up to capture the scene's atmosphere. Reportedly, there were as many as seven takes of the scene, and because of Crosby and Hope's propensity to add unwritten lines, for each take there were never fewer than five pages of dialogue recorded by the overworked script girl.

Whether scripted or ad-libbed, many of the lines were genuinely funny. In one scene Crosby and Hope come across a deserted tribal burial ground in a conelike clay structure. Amidst a number of skeletons attached to wooden stakes are a multitude of various sized drums. Crosby decides to try sending messages via the native drums in a Morse code fashion.

> Crosby: "Any messages for the folks?"
> Hope: "Can you send over 10 words?"
> Crosby beats out a rhythm.
> Hope: "What was that?"
> Crosby: "I just sent it collect."

Another segment in the film features humorous subtitles for the primitive king and local witch doctor as they speak in their native tongue.

"You may think they're gods, but I think they're a couple of phoney-baloney's," read the witch doctor's subtitles on the screen.

"Sam says they're gods and that's good enough for me," replied the king, via subtitles.

"That's a lotta hooey," read the subtitles while the foreign dialect was heard. "If he's a god ... I'm Mickey Mouse."

Even the one-liners are plentiful. When the two stranded adventurers stumble across the aforementioned deserted tribal burial ground

Chuck Reardon (Bing Crosby) and Fearless Frazier (Bob Hope) regale in the royalty bestowed upon them as a native tribe treats them as gods in *Road to Zanzibar* **(1941).**

with the skeletons strewn about, Hope shakes a skeleton's bony hand and says: "Don't get up."

In a later scene, Hope and Crosby are detained in primitive cages as the cannibal tribe eagerly prepares them for dinner. A cannibal native saunters by and lets out a burp. Hope says: "It must have been somebody he ate."

As with *Singapore*, the set of *Zanzibar* was crazy and unmanageable, with Hope and Crosby leaving Lamour in the wake of their spirited banter. Still, every once in a while Lamour got her revenge. During one rehearsal she remained very tight-lipped while Hope and Crosby shot lines back and forth. The scene ended with both of them turning to her and saying, "How about it?" Lamour smiled demurely, and the two principals fell over with laughter. Makeup man Harry Ray had blacked out two of Lamour's front teeth.

But as far as the laughs on the screen were concerned, Lamour was always going to finish a distant third, and she knew it. But being a former Miss New Orleans more than made up for her lack of laugh lines. The audiences would hear the Hope-Crosby banter, but see much more of Lamour, because she was always dressed in a very revealing costume.

It seemed that Paramount had a slogan, "show as much of Lamour as the censors will permit—with or without the sarong." To that end, the script of *Zanzibar* included Lamour taking a bath in the nude (actually wearing a flesh-colored bathing suit) and two leopards stealing her clothes so she is forced to cover up with whatever is near at hand. On May 7, 1941, the Hollywood cameramen voted Lamour one of the "Ten Best Undressed Women" for her appearance "clad only in a handful of ferns ... in Paramount's *Road to Zanzibar*." Naturally, the ads featured pictures of Lamour in fernwear along with the line, "Bob and Bing take a tour with Lamour through brightest Africa ... and it's touriffic!"

Lamour was a perfect balance for the likes of Hope and Crosby. They loved to tease her, and she always took it in stride. In the scene in *Zanzibar* in which Lamour sings "You're Dangerous" to Hope, the two are supposed to sit on a log together in the middle of the song. Lamour, clad in a short-sleeved white blouse and short skirt, came in, started her song, and then sat down on the log, but immediately jumped back up. Hope yelled, "Cut! Get me a barber!" Crosby said, "Why cut? Why a barber?" Hope explained, "We need a barber to shave this log. Miss Lamour's sitter is much too sensitive to sit on this rough log."

Even director Schertzinger got into the act. His style and congeniality were apparent in his relationship to the actors when not filming. On occasion, he would have as much fun as the rest of the cast and crew. When a flu epidemic hit during *Zanzibar,* a sign was made with the names Schertzinger, Merkel, Crosby, Lamour, and Hope on it. Beside each name was the individual's current temperature, and the one with the lowest reading was required to buy lunch. Hope lost.

In some ways, *Zanzibar* is a better picture than *Singapore* because the entire film is played for laughs and there is less emphasis on the musical aspects of the movie. This trend would continue in the "Road" films until *Road to Rio* in 1947.

The billing for *Road to Zanzibar* and the rest of the series films was also more firmly established, reflecting the accent on comedy. Lamour, who received second billing in *Singapore*, is third to Crosby and Hope, respectively, in *Zanzibar*. This was more indicative of Hope's rising status than anything else.

In *Road to Zanzibar*, Hope and Crosby began to depart, ever so

Donna Latour (Dorothy Lamour) takes comfort in the arm of Chuck Reardon (Bing Crosby) as Fearless Frazier (Bob Hope) looks on in the 1941 film *Road to Zanzibar*.

slightly, from the ordinary confines of the script. Still, aside from references to the patty-cake routine from *Singapore*, nothing is outside the frame of the plot, and none of the action is supernatural.

That changed with *Road to Morocco*.

Road to Zanzibar
A Paramount Picture

Released: April 1941
Running Time: 92 minutes

Producer Paul Jones; *Assistant Producer* David Hire; *Production Secretaries* Marie Morris, Marg Potts; *Director* Victor Schertzinger; *1st Assistant Director* Hal Walker; *2d Assistant Director* Alvin Ganzer; *Directorial Secretary* Eleanore Edwards; *Screenplay by* Frank Butler and Don Hartman; *Based on a story by* Don Hartman and Sy Bartlett; *Dialogue Director* R. Gallaher; *Script Clerk* Laprele Jones; *Director of Photography* Ted Tetzlaff; *Second Cameraman* Daniel Fapp; *Second Unit*

Cameraman Haskell Boggs; *Art Direction* Hans Dreier and Robert Usher; *Editor* Alma Macrorie; *Costumes* Edith Head; *Wardrobe Men* Mickey Cohen, J. Wade; *Wardrobe Women* Ruth Davis, Harriett Altman; *Sound Recording* Earl Hayman and Don Johnson; *Musical Director* Victor Young; *Musical Adviser* Arthur Franklin; *Song Lyrics by* Johnny Burke; *Music by* Jimmy Van Heusen; *Musical Numbers staged by* LeRoy Prinz; *Assistant Dance Directors* Edward Prinz, J. Crosby; *Dance Secretary* Hazel Noe; *Unit Manager* D. Keefe; *Property Men* R. Keueger, Jimmy Cottrell, and Bob Goodstein; *Location Manager* N. Lacey; *Set Dresser* George Sawley; *Supervisory Set Dresser* Sam Comer; *Hairdresser* Merle Reeves; *Hairdressing Supervisor* Leonora Sabine; *Makeup Artist* Harry Ray; *Makeup Supervisor* Wally Westmore.

CAST

Chuck Reardon	Bing Crosby
Hubert "Fearless" Frazier	Bob Hope
Donna Latour	Dorothy Lamour
Julia Quimby	Una Merkel
Charles Kimble	Eric Blore
Slave Trader	Douglass Dumbrille
French Soubrette in Cafe	Iris Adrian
Monsieur Lebec	Lionel Royce
Thonga	Buck Woods
Scarface	Leigh Whipper
Whiteface	Ernest Whitman
Chief	Noble Johnson
Boy	Leo Gorcey
Dimples	Joan Marsh
Proprietor of Native Booth	Luis Alberni
Police Inspector	Robert Middlemass
Clara Kimble	Norma Varden
Turk at Slave Market	Paul Porcasi
Fat Lady	Ethel Loreen Greer
Saunders	Georges Renavent
Soloman	Jules Strongbow
Curzon Sisters—Iron Jaw Act	Priscilla White
	LaVerne Vess
Acrobats	Harry C. Johnson
	Harry C. Johnson, Jr.
Policeman	Alan Bridge
Proprietor in Cafe	Henry Roquemore
Waiter in Cafe	James B. Carson
Barber	Eddy Conrad
Clerk	Richard Keene
Gorilla	Charlie Gemora
Commentator	Ken Carpenter

Road to Morocco, 1942

Many a hopeful actor has felt the harsh sting of the proverbial spit in the face from Hollywood. But few, however, have experienced that kind of treatment while on the set of a movie—and from an animal, no less.

By the time *Road to Morocco* was released in 1942, the freewheeling comedic nature of Bing Crosby and Bob Hope appeared to be catching. In one of the opening scenes, a despondent Hope and Crosby sit on a sandy beach analyzing their fate. From behind some bushes, a camel ambles up and licks each of them on their faces. The two travelers turn around to find the dromedary standing there, and they move towards it, planning to catch a ride on the beast. But as Hope approaches the animal's head, the humpbacked creature turns and spits in the comedian's face. Stunned by the unexpectedness of the spit and its foul odor, Hope loses his footing and stumbles out of the scene. "Print that," said David Butler, the director. "We'll leave it in." It was so spontaneous that it was left in the final cut of the film.

By the time filming for *Morocco* started, everyone involved with the series knew that spontaneity was becoming a trademark of the "Road" pictures. Because of Victor Schertzinger's gently guiding hand in the first two films, Butler, Hope, and Crosby knew with certainty that, if nothing else, a "Road" picture meant something unplanned was bound to happen.

"If anything happened that was out of the ordinary, I'd always let the camera run," said Butler. "And we got some of our funniest stuff after the scene was over. I'd let the camera roll until they got off the set, or walked out, or whatever happened."

Increased spontaneity captured on film was only one new facet that the third "Road" picture displayed. *Morocco* was the first film of the series to incorporate supernatural action and the first of the "Road" series to consistently use references outside the plot of the film, some of which started at the beginning of the movie.

Early in the film, Crosby and Hope are singing the title song while traveling through the desert in a jarring fashion on camelback. Through the course of the song there emerge such references as "I'll lay you eight to five we'll meet Dorothy Lamour" and "Paramount will protect us 'cause we're signed for five more years."

Towards the end of the film, when Hope and Crosby are sequestered in a desert jail, Hope paces back and forth as he explains the plot in detail. A bewildered Crosby, sitting off to the side at the jail's barred window, says, "I know that."

"Yeah, but the people who came in the middle of the picture don't," said Hope.

"You mean they missed my song?" gasps Crosby.

Then in the final scene of the picture, Crosby, Hope, Lamour, and Dona Drake are floating on the remains of an exploded ship. Crosby stands in short pants and ragged shirt, and Hope appears in tattered pants and assorted fragments of a coat and tie. Hope is emotionally pleading to be spared from death and saved from the shipwreck but is interrupted by Crosby. Hope chides Crosby for interfering by saying: "You had to open your big mouth and ruin the only good scene I've got in the picture. I might have won an Academy Award."

On occasion, references outside the plot gave the writers plenty of freedom. When Hope asks how he and Crosby escaped from netted sacks while stranded in the middle of the desert, Crosby says: "If we told anybody, they'd never believe it." Hope replies: "Oh, let's not tell them, huh."

Other lines were more predictable, but just as amusing. At one point in the film, bad guy Anthony Quinn, dressed in white and silver sheik's clothing complete with flowing turban and cape, threatens Crosby and calls him a "moonfaced son of a one-eyed donkey," to which Hope advises Crosby: "I wouldn't let him call me that even if there *is* a resemblance."

In another scene, Hope and Lamour are talking about Crosby and whether they like him or not.

"I think he's one of the nicest men I've ever met," says Lamour tenderly.

Bob Hope, Dorothy Lamour, and Bing Crosby take a breather on the set of
Road to Morocco, **the third picture in the "Road" series, made in 1942.**

"Oh, he's a nice fellow as nice fellows go," says Hope, "and why
don't he."

Most of the banter between Hope and Crosby in *Morocco* was
typical of the first two films. In one scene, Hope feigns disinterest in
Arab handmaiden Dona Drake's embraces and says: "Later. You know
you gotta catch me when I'm in the mood for that sort of thing." Crosby
responds, "You ain't been out of it for 20 years."

In this third "Road" picture, Jeff Peters (Crosby) and Orville "Turkey" Jackson (Hope) land in Morocco after a shipwreck, and as usual, they are broke. While in Morocco, Crosby casually sells Hope into slavery to pay for a dinner check. Later, Crosby dreams about Hope's plight and is chastised in the dream by Hope's Aunt Lucy (played predictably by Hope with wire-rimmed glasses, a high bonnet, long curled wig, and high-pitched, staccato voice). Crosby, appropriately contrite, sets off to find Hope and learns he has become headman at the desert paradise of Princess Shalimar (Lamour).

Hope, however, is unaware that he is being set up to fulfill a prophecy of a fortune teller. The prophet has informed Lamour that her first marriage is doomed to be short and dismal, with her husband meeting a violent death. When Crosby enters the royal palace of the princess, Lamour, not surprisingly, falls for him, even though she is betrothed to desert prince Mullay Kasim (Quinn) for her second marriage. Quinn does not take kindly to Crosby's or Hope's intervention and eventually carts off Lamour and Drake to his desert encampment. The boys subsequently infiltrate Quinn's sand-filled campsite to rescue the girls via dribble glasses, hot feet, and, in essence, a whoopee cushion.

The critical notices for *Road to Morocco* were mixed, but most of the critics, as well as the public, liked the film.

The *New York Times* hailed it a hit. "It is, in short, a lampoon of all pictures having to do with exotic romance, played by a couple of wise guys who can make a gag do everything but lay an egg." *Variety* saw it as "a bubbly spontaneous entertainment without a semblance of sanity."

But some critics thought it was a bit crude. Howard Barnes of the *Herald Tribune* flatly denounced the movie as decadent. "Paramount has been teetering on the edge of antic vulgarity in several Bing Crosby, Bob Hope, Dorothy Lamour 'Road' pictures. It takes a nose dive with *Road to Morocco*," he declared angrily. Barnes went on to predict that despite its alleged pandering to bad taste, the film would almost certainly be a huge hit. On that point he was right.

Part of the film's success can once again be attributed to the fine supporting cast. In *Road to Morocco*, Anthony Quinn was back to play an intimidating force in the lives of Hope, Crosby, and Lamour. In *Morocco*, Quinn played a larger role than he did in *Road to Singapore*, partly because of his increased status as a rising actor. He also was more glamorous than in *Singapore*, donning exotic Arab robes and headdresses and becoming an even more formidable foe.

Bob Hope and Dorothy Lamour appear to be getting some vocal assistance from an unidentified visitor between scenes on the set of *Road to Morocco*.

In addition to Quinn, *Morocco* boasted a newcomer, Yvonne De-Carlo. She would go on to appear in epics such as *The Ten Commandments* (1956), but would gain more fame as Lily on the television series *The Munsters*.

Other cast members in *Road to Morocco* included Vladimir Sokoloff, Mikhail Rasumny, and George Givot. Nestor Paiva had a bit part

**Jeff Peters (Bing Crosby) is skeptical of Turkey Jackson (Bob Hope) in the
third picture in the "Road" series, *Road to Morocco*, released in 1942.**

but would play more prominent roles in *Road to Utopia* and *Road to Rio*.
Monte Blue also played a bit part.

　　Road to Morocco is a frenzied spoof of the multitude of Arab and
sheik movies made in Hollywood in the late twenties and early thirties.
But the film is lackluster and, at times, slow moving. Played mostly for
laughs, it contains few musical numbers and none of the vaudevillian-
type antics of the first two pictures. (It does, however, give Hope more
of a chance to shine with some physical comedy including a bit where
he and Crosby are escaping Quinn by pretending to be head-nodding
statues. When a fly pesters Hope unmercifully, he grimaces and reacts
with a multitude of facial gestures.)

　　But the tried and true patty-cake routine is there—almost. In one
scene, Quinn is about to take Lamour and Drake away from Lamour's
palace when Crosby and Hope start in on the patty-cake bit. Just as
they are about to land their blows on their victim, Quinn bumps their
heads together and they go sprawling into a grassy knoll.

　　"Yes sir, Junior," Crosby says to Hope as they get up and brush
themselves off, "that thing sure got around!"

Mullay Kasim (Anthony Quinn) is momentarily fooled by Jeff Peters (Bing Crosby) and Turkey Jackson (Bob Hope) who pose as statues in the 1942 film *Road to Morocco.*

"Yeah, and back to us," responds Hope.

According to Lamour, Quinn's resemblance to Rudolph Valentino was not lost on Frank Butler and Don Hartman, the writers of *Road to Morocco.* Veteran actor Monte Blue, who had worked with Valentino, had a bit part in *Road to Morocco* and told Quinn he looked remarkably like the silent-screen star. "The writers obviously agreed," said Lamour, "because they wrote one scene in which Tony kidnaps me and gallops away over the sand dunes, very much like Valentino and Agnes Ayres in *The Sheik.*"

But scenes and screenplays did not always come so easily to Butler and Hartman. The two writers had a basic contract with Paramount which paid them a modest yearly salary, but if they came up with an original story idea, they would be paid extra. Always on the lookout for a little more cash, the two screenwriters stayed up late one night and devised a plot for a film they called "Road to Moscow." Although they had nothing on paper, Buddy DeSylva, the songwriter who had become head of the studio, gave the two neophyte scribes a chance to peddle their idea one day in his office.

Hartman, the storyteller of the two, got up and ad-libbed the entire movie. DeSylva started laughing and that encouraged Hartman to improvise even more. DeSylva kept chuckling throughout Hartman's spirited presentation and when Hartman finished, he told the two writers to get to work and write the screenplay. DeSylva wholeheartedly assured them that "Road to Moscow" would be the next "Road" picture.

Excited by their triumph, Hartman and Butler again stayed up all night, this time to celebrate. The next day, when trying to write the story they had told DeSylva the day before, they came up empty. Hartman could barely remember what he had said in DeSylva's office, and Butler had not bothered to take notes. Finally, Butler asked, "What was Buddy laughing so loud at?"

"I don't know," said Hartman. "I was selling so hard, I wasn't listening to what I was saying."

After several more attempts to come up with a story, a discouraged Butler finally gave up. "We'll have to go to Buddy and ask him to tell us what we sold him," he said.

So they went to DeSylva's office, and Hartman contritely explained that on occasion he got so involved in telling a story that he sometimes ad-libbed and then forgot most of what he had said.

"I know it was great and you enjoyed it so much," said Hartman, "but could you please tell us what parts of the story you were laughing so hard at?"

And DeSylva told them, "I was laughing so hard because you guys had come up with such a lousy story, you were going to have to break your butts to get a screenplay out of it."

They never did. "Road to Moscow" was never made but, fortunately, Butler and Hartman did pen the first three "Road" pictures.

They were so adept at the "Road" formula by this time that in 1942 an Academy Award nomination for writing an original screenplay went to Frank Butler and Don Hartman for *Road to Morocco*. The award that year, however, went to Michael Kanin and Ring Lardner, Jr., for *Woman of the Year*.

With the success of the first two "Roads," Paramount wanted film audiences to be ready and waiting for the third "Road" picture when it was released. The publicity department came up with several gimmicks, one of which was attaching a series of cards to the drinking fountains in the towns where the film was playing. They read: "Thirsty for entertainment?—See what happens when Bob Hope chases Bing Crosby and Dorothy Lamour to a desert oasis on the *Road to Morocco*."

Bob Hope clowns with an unexpected visitor on the set of *Road to Morocco*.

But there was one chase during the filming of *Morocco* that almost turned out disastrous, at least as far as the two leads were concerned.

An ex-actor and ex-stuntman, director David Butler believed actors should do their own stunts whenever possible. He shot a scene in *Road to Morocco* in which Crosby and Hope are casually walking down a narrow street and then suddenly find themselves being chased through the village by about thirty Arabian horsemen. The two stars, dressed in casual khaki slacks, sport shirts, and sailor caps, were supposed to see the horsemen coming a half-mile away and start walking quickly, then break into a trot, then into a run. Just as the raiders' horses were about to pass over the spot where Hope and Crosby were standing, Butler was supposed to holler over the loudspeaker so the two stars could jump out of the way of the oncoming horses.

The comedic pair started walking through the narrow street of rug merchants and pottery peddlers, and as the horses loomed closer, the two stars began running but never heard anything from Butler. When both thought they were no longer safe from being trampled, Hope jumped through an open doorway, while Crosby cascaded through a window.

"Great shot," said Butler as the two stars dusted themselves off and attended to any wounds sustained during the incident.

"Great shot?" said an incredulous Crosby. "You almost killed us!"

"Oh, I wouldn't do that," said Butler calmly. "Not until the final scene, anyway."

A major film star for ten years on the silent screen, Butler turned to directing in 1927 and became one of Hollywood's most successful directors at Fox, RKO, Paramount, and Warner Bros. He specialized in musical comedies and his film credits include Shirley Temple's *The Little Colonel* (1935) and *My Wild Irish Rose* (1947). Butler had theatrical background even in his youth because his father was a stage director.

The heavyset Butler was a serious and exacting director. His days in the Mack Sennett rough-and-tumble silent films enabled him to anticipate and deal with the unexpected. Probably because of Butler's silent comedy training, *Morocco* was filled with outrageous sight gags.

At one point in the picture, Hope's curve-toed Arab shoes become uncurled when Lamour kisses him passionately. "Now kiss him on the nose," Crosby suggests. "See if you can straighten that out."

The same dromedary that earlier spat in Hope's face had a line of its own, thanks to special effects. After a scene of rival Arab camps being subjected to dribble glasses and exploding cigarettes, a close-up shot of the camel shows it saying, "This is the screwiest picture I was ever in." Other special effects displays included a mirage scene in the desert for a reprise of "Moonlight Becomes You" in which the three stars lip-sync to each other's voices, with hilarious results.

In yet another scene altered by special effects, Hope and Crosby are in a desert jail and Lamour sends them a magic ring which grants three wishes. Not believing in such nonsense, Hope, dressed in a flowing silk shirt, embroidered vest, and embroidered slacks, wishes he had a drink. Suddenly, a tall, cool glass appears in his hand. He is so surprised that he says, "I'll be a monkey's uncle" and of course turns into a monkey wearing the exact same outfit. The third wish brings him back.

While setting up the scene, Butler told Crosby he had to stand perfectly still so they could match the shot of Hope and Crosby with the next shot of Crosby and the monkey.

"Don't worry, Dave," said Crosby. "You're making a monkey out of Ski Nose and you think I won't stand still for that? Try me, brother, I'll be a real statue."

As confounding and difficult as Hope and Crosby might have been filming a scene, they were no easier to handle on the set when the cameras weren't rolling. The cunning Butler tried to maneuver the two wanderers into putting in a good day's worth of work by eliminating interruptions.

Butler knew Crosby and Hope spent much of their studio time talking on the telephone discussing their radio shows, investments, and other matters. Butler, however, wanted the duo's full attention.

In those days there was only one telephone on a movie set, and Butler arranged to position the phone for *Road to Morocco* a block and a half away from the set where they were working. To make it even more inconvenient, the telephone was installed under a large pile of construction lumber so that anyone answering it would have to slide in horizontally to pick up the receiver. Butler thought the arrangement would cut down on the active twosome's trips to the telephone while the picture was being shot.

Butler's plan worked well until one day when producer Sam Goldwyn called to talk to Butler. The call came at a time when Butler was directing a crowd scene which involved a multitude of animals and several hundred people. He had to tell the company to wait while he trudged across the vast soundstage and into the next one and clumsily slid under the pile of lumber.

Goldwyn was working on the script that Butler was going to direct next—for Hope, as it turned out. For 15 minutes, Goldwyn went on and on about the story while the *Road to Morocco* company waited. Finally Goldwyn, who apparently thought Butler had originated the call, said, "Thanks very much for calling me," and hung up. Butler's planned nuisance for Hope and Crosby had inconvenienced himself as well.

Bob Hope clowns with a studio executive on the set of *Road to Morocco*.

The costuming for *Road to Morocco* also was an inconvenience, at least for one of the stars. Hope and Lamour did not mind the time it took to get into their exotic attire, but Crosby hated dressing up. Edith Head, Paramount's Oscar-winning costume designer, said Crosby almost always complained about wearing the jeweled caftans and turbans, but Hope was enthusiastic. "He'd put on a turban and be amused by it," she said of the comedian.

But the costuming also provided another opportunity for the verbal sparring. Hope was dressed in some fancy robes, turban, and sashes, and Crosby accused him of gaining weight.

"After this picture," Crosby said to Hope, "you're going to be known as the man with the balloons fore and aft."

"Well," replied Hope, "you've always been best known as the little fat man who sings."

"Maybe," laughed Crosby, "but right now you look like a pile of old, tired laundry."

Hope quickly replied, "And you look like the bag for it."

By this time the two stars' quick-witted banter was well established, and the kidding continued off the set as well. When they recorded the song "We're Off on the Road to Morocco" together for Decca Records, Hope was quick with a reference to Crosby's competitor, a young Frank Sinatra.

"That's a pretty good tenor you sang for me," said Crosby after the recording session. "Why don't you leave your name at the door?"

"I think I'd better team up with Sinatra," countered Hope, "he's a little younger. More my speed."

After their songwriting success with *Road to Zanzibar*, Jimmy Van Heusen and Johnny Burke were assigned to work on *Road to Morocco*. They scored again with the popular Crosby ballad "Moonlight Becomes You" and the whimsical "Ain't Got a Dime to My Name," also by Crosby. In addition to the title tune, songs in the film included Lamour's "Constantly." The songwriting team of Burke and Van Heusen also would work on the next three "Road" films: *Utopia*, *Rio* and *Bali*.

The cinema travelers had now completed three "Road" films, all of which were set in contemporary time frames. But in order to keep things fresh for filmgoers, that aspect changed with the next "Road" film. *Road to Utopia* was a period piece set in the 1890s, told almost entirely in flashback.

Road to Morocco
A Paramount Picture

Released: October 1942
Running time: 83 minutes

Associate Producer Paul Jones; *Production Assistant* H. Schwartz; *Production Secretary* Marie Morris; *Director* David Butler; *Assistant*

Director Hal Walker; *2d Assistant Director* Bob Adams; *Co-Director* H. Tate; *Original Screenplay by* Frank Butler and Don Hartman; *Script Clerk* Laprele Jones; *Director of Photography* William C. Mellor; *Second Cameraman* Neal Beckner; *Art Direction* Hans Dreier and Robert Odell; *Special Effects Supervisor* Gordon Jennings; *Transparency Supervisor* Farciot Edouart; *Edited by* Irene Morra; *Costumes by* Edith Head; *Wardrobe Man* Mickey Cohen; *Wardrobe Woman* Ruth Davis; *Instructor or Coach* Francis Dawson; *Musical Direction* Victor Young; *Music Adviser* Arthur Franklin; *Song Lyrics by* Johnny Burke; *Music by* James Van Heusen; *Sound Recording by* Earl Hartman and Walter Oberst; *Dances Staged by* Paul Oscard; *Dance Supervisor* S. Ledner; *Assistant Dance Director* Bob Goodstein; *Assistant Dance Director* Al Mann; *Makeup Artist* Wally Westmore; *Hairdressing Supervision* Leonora Sabine; *Horse Wrangler* William Hurley; *Property Men* J. Thompson and Jimmy Cottrell; *Unit Manager* S. Street;. *Technical Adviser* C. Hassan; *Set Dresser* Ray Moyer; *Supervisory Set Dresser* Sam Comer

CAST

Jeff Peters	Bing Crosby
Turkey Jackson	Bob Hope
Princess Shalimar	Dorothy Lamour
Mullay Kasim	Anthony Quinn
Mihirmah	Dona Drake
Ahmed Fey	Mikhail Rasumny
Hyder Khan	Vladimir Sokoloff
Neb Jolla	George Givot
Oso Bucco	Andrew Tombes
Yusef	Leon Belasco
Aides to Mullay Kasim	Jamiel Hasson
	Monte Blue
Handmaiden	Louise LaPlanche
Handmaiden	Theo de Voe
Handmaiden	Brooke Evans
Handmaiden	Suzanne Ridgway
Handmaiden	Patsy Mace
Handmaiden	Yvonne DeCarlo
Handmaiden	Poppy Wilde
1st Guard	George Lloyd
2d Guard	Sammy Stein
Arabian Waiter	Ralph Penney
Arabian Buyer	Dan Seymour
Philippine Announcer	Pete G. Katchenaro
English Announcer	Brandon Hurst
Chinese Announcer	Richard Loo
Russian Announcer	Leo Mostovoy

Knife Dancers	Vic Groves
	Joe Jewett
Arab Pottery Vendor	Michael Mark
Arab Sausage Vendor	Nestor Paiva
Idiot	Stanley Price
Specialty Dancer	Rita Christiani
Gigantic Bearded Arab	Robert Barron
Arab Booth Proprietor	Cy Kendall
Voice of Lady Camel	Sara Berner
Voice of Man Camel	Kent Rogers
Warriors	Harry Cording
	Dick Botiller
Bystander	Edward Emerson
Dancer	Sylvia Opert

Road to Utopia, 1945

For avid filmgoers accustomed to the distinctive good looks of Bing Crosby, the charming and chiseled features of Bob Hope, and the glamour of Dorothy Lamour in the movies of the mid–1940s, the opening scene of *Road to Utopia* probably came as quite a shock.

After a brief introduction by humorist Robert Benchley, the movie opens with Hope and Lamour seated by the fire in the parlor of their luxurious mansion enjoying their elderly life together. They appear, through makeup wizardry, to be in their seventies, complete with white hair, glasses, and wrinkles.

The doorbell sounds, and Crosby, also made up to look about 70, ambles in with two lovely and enticing young women. Hope and Lamour are surprised to see him, because they left him for dead nearly 35 years earlier, and thus starts the flashback story of Alaska and the Gold Rush era of the 1890s. *Road to Utopia* was the only "Road" in the series not set in current times.

In *Utopia*, Crosby plays Duke Johnson and Hope plays Chester Hooton, a couple of vaudevillian con men performing a magic/money-changing act in San Francisco at the turn of the century. As in previous films, Crosby portrays the shill and the barker, while Hope represents the unwilling participant in the sham. Their con game is revealed, and again they are on the lam and on the road. This time Crosby tricks Hope into traveling to Alaska to search for gold. As Crosby says in the film: "It's Utopia. Everybody is gettin' some of that gold on 'em."

While working their way across the ocean on a ship by mopping decks, stoking coal, and cleaning cabins, they come across a stolen map which two murderers indirectly stole from Skagway Sal (Lamour). Hope

Duke Johnson (Bing Crosby), Sal (Dorothy Lamour), and Chester Hooton (Bob Hope) in the opening scene of *Road to Utopia* (1945).

and Crosby take on the vicious identities of the two murderers and spend most of the picture pursuing Lamour, avoiding the two killers, and trying to outsmart an unscrupulous tavern owner (Douglass Dumbrille), who is also seeking the gold mine map.

Reviews of the fourth "Road" film were generally good, with *Variety* calling it "a zany laugh-getter," but also saying that the songs "were not of a heavy caliber." The critic may have missed the mark a bit on the songs, however, as Johnny Burke and Jimmy Van Heusen were back for the songwriting duties and turned in some fine work.

"Put It There, Pal" became a Crosby-Hope theme song and Lamour's double-entendre song "Personality" pushed the limits to which bawdy verbal humor was being introduced into film at that time.

Other songs included "Good Time Charley" (in which Hope and Crosby harmonize nicely), Crosby's "It's Anybody's Spring," and Lamour's "Would You." Crosby's ballad "Welcome to My Dream" became a hit.

In supporting roles, the *Road to Utopia* showcased the talents of stern-faced character actor Douglass Dumbrille. Through his career

Dumbrille appeared in more than 250 films, playing lawyers, senators, villains, judges, tycoons, and fathers.

No stranger to comedy, Dumbrille appeared with the Marx Brothers in *A Day at the Races* (1937) and *The Big Store* (1941). He also annoyed Abbott and Costello in *Ride 'em Cowboy* (1942), *Lost in a Harem* (1944), and *Abbott and Costello in the Foreign Legion* (1950). In addition to trading insults with Hope in *Road to Utopia*, Dumbrille appeared in Hope's *Monsieur Beaucaire* (1946) and *Son of Paleface* (1952) as well as *Road to Morocco*. Dumbrille also exuded his nastiness in several Jeanette MacDonald/Nelson Eddy films including *Naughty Marietta* (1935), *The Firefly* (1937), and *I Married an Angel* (1942). He also appeared in *Mr. Deeds Goes to Town* (1936) and several Charlie Chan films.

Road to Utopia also boasted the talents of Robert Benchley and his dry narration. Benchley was a humorist who very often viewed life through a tilted cocktail glass. When he was not writing for the *New Yorker* magazine, he appeared in such films as *I Married a Witch* and *The Major and the Minor*, both in 1942.

Other actors in the film are Hillary Brooke, Jack La Rue, Robert Barrat, Nestor Paiva (who appeared in *Road to Morocco* and also would play a role in the next "Road" film, *Road to Rio*), Will Wright, and Jimmy Dundee.

Road to Utopia was the only picture in the series that was a costume piece. In addition to that slight change, other minor alterations were occurring in the film series. *Road to Utopia* was the first "Road" to be made without writing founders Don Hartman and Frank Butler. This time the screenplay was written by Hope's former radio gag writers, Norman Panama and Mel Frank. The only information the two writers were given was that the picture was to be set in Alaska during the Gold Rush era. Although they had several unique ideas for the film, the two writers had to convince the three stars that their concepts would work.

At that time, Crosby, Hope, and Lamour were enormous stars at Paramount, and the two writers obtained their permission for any ideas they might use. This was a courtesy more than anything else because all three stars were under contract and technically could be forced to do what was wanted of them.

The screenwriters first sat down with Crosby and explained the story to him so it sounded like it was going to be a Bing Crosby picture. Then they told Hope the story so it sounded attractive from his point of view. Then, of course, they told it to Dorothy Lamour. Not surprisingly, all three bought the Panama-Frank story line without reservations.

The alteration in the behind-the-scene personnel may have dictated other changes in this, the fourth "Road" of the series. Benchley's running bit in *Utopia* had him appear in the corner of the screen and comment, in a pretentious manner, on what was occurring in the film. For example, early on in the movie when an elderly man is being murdered, the film stops and Benchley appears in the frame and states, "Now this is a device known as the flashback." At another interval, when there are hundreds of extras milling around a shipping dock area, the film stops and he comments, "This seems to be a scene they put in after I saw the picture at the studio." Still later in the film, when about ten chorus girls are dancing on stage in a tavern and waving their dresses with a flourish, the film is halted and Benchley quips, "Now at this point the plot is much more interesting from your point of view than mine."

By the time the fourth "Road" film was ready to be made, music had been relegated to a secondary position behind comedy. That may have been part of the reason the *Road to Utopia* was directed by Hal Walker, a veteran director of comedic films. (He also directed the sixth film in the series, *Road to Bali.*)

Some of Walker's early comedy-film directing included *Out of this World* (1944), in which Eddie Bracken plays a crooning telegram boy whose life becomes complicated when he hitches up with a stranded all-girl orchestra. The big gag in this film was that whenever Bracken opened his mouth and sang, Crosby's voice was heard. Walker also directed a potpourri of stars in *Duffy's Tavern* (1945), loosely inspired by the radio show of the same name.

After *Utopia* and before *Bali*, Walker directed four Dean Martin and Jerry Lewis films: *My Friend Irma Goes West* and *At War with the Army* (both 1950), and *That's My Boy* and *Sailor Beware* (both 1951). Walker left films to use his comedic expertise in television by directing the *I Married Joan* series from 1952 to 1955. *I Married Joan* was a domestic sitcom starring Joan Davis as Joan Stevens and Jim Backus as her husband, Judge Bradley Stevens.

But for all his comedic directing ability, Walker did not add much to the "Road" series. In both *Utopia* and *Bali*, the characters are already well defined, the plots are basic, and the gags are already established. Much of the humor for *Utopia* was derived from dialogue and quick quips, especially since screenwriters Panama and Frank had done considerable writing for radio.

At one point early in the film, Crosby and Hope are saying goodbye to each other at the shipping docks. Crosby, clothed in a dark suit, derby, and tie, says to Hope, "Chester, we had a couple of things that money couldn't buy." "Yeah," says Hope, in a straw hat, light-colored suit, and double-breasted vest, "and I usually got the ugly one."

Later in the film, the two men are cloaked in heavy plaid coats with fur collars and fur hats as they travel the frozen terrain by dogsled. Hope is giving a speech about swearing off women forever.

"Oh, they're poison," says Hope, standing on the rear of the dogsled. "They run their fingers through your hair, play with your ear, roll ya, clip ya, and then they throw ya in the gutter. You know what's worse than that?"

"What?" asks Crosby, seated in the sled.

Hope replies, "I love it."

In another scene, Hope and Crosby are spying on Lamour through a window as she earnestly explains to the bad guys that she is in love with either the crooner or the comedian.

"Imagine a girl lovin' a guy that much," says Crosby, crouched down in front of Hope.

"Yeah, I'm not worth it," comments Hope. "I'm a regular Casablanca."

"Casanova," corrects Crosby.

Hope, a bit bewildered, says, "When did they change that?"

Although the humor comes off effortlessly, Mel Frank thinks gag writing is the most difficult form of communication. "The actual art of writing gags is one of the sharpest forms of creation that I know of. It's like writing novels in terms of telegrams. Gags are stories; you have to use the right words, the right thoughts, and in a very small period of time say things that are going to make people laugh."

Frank was responsible for a *Utopia* line which became a movie classic. In *Road to Utopia*, Hope and Crosby had to act tough to impress the local bad guys. They saunter up to a bar in the mining town, and the head heavy asks, "What'll you have?"

"Oh, a couple of fingers of rotgut," growls Crosby.

"What's yours?" asks Douglass Dumbrille.

"I'll take a lemonade," squeaks Hope in a high-pitched voice before responding to a nudge by Crosby and snarling, "in a dirty glass."

The quick wit and surefire gags did not go unnoticed. Norman

Panama and Melvin Frank received an Academy Award nomination in 1946 for writing the original screenplay of *Road to Utopia*. But the competition that year was fierce. They were up against Ben Hecht for *Notorious* and eventually lost to Muriel Box and Sydney Box for *The Seventh Veil*.

As humorous as the dialogue was, the supernatural effects of the previous film were not abandoned entirely for *Utopia*. Effects scribed by writers Panama and Frank included a talking fish and a talking bear. In addition, the writers were wise enough to retain the tried and true bits of references outside the plot, much to the fans' delight. An example of the references outside the plot lunacy occurs early in the film when Crosby arrives at Hope's home. "And I thought this was going to be an 'A' picture," Hope complains to the audience.

Later in the film the up-to-date references continue. While crossing the arctic wastelands in the aforementioned dogsled, the pair see a familiar-looking mountain in the distance. "Bread and butter," Hope remarks. "That's a mountain," Crosby corrects. "Looks like bread and butter to me," Hope insists as the mountain takes on a halo of stars that duplicates the Paramount Pictures trademark.

When Hope and Crosby are stripped down to slacks and undershirts while stoking coal in a ship's boiler room, a man in a full-dress tuxedo and top hat walks past.

"Are you in this picture?" asks Crosby.

"No. Taking a short-cut to Stage 10," says the man.

When Crosby loses an amateur night contest to a monkey and his trainer, Hope quips, "Next time I bring Sinatra."

But for all the good humor, some things were definitely lacking in *Utopia*. For the first time, there was no patty-cake routine performed by Hope and Crosby. Instead, there is a variation on the theme with the rug literally being pulled out from under their victims. It is effective, but not nearly as funny as the innocuous and simple-minded patty-cake masterpiece.

Also, having a narrator slowed things down a bit. As funny as humorist Robert Benchley could be, at times he seemed out of place. His comments are comical bits in and of themselves, but they sometimes interfere with the flow of the picture.

One of the best things to come out of *Utopia*, however, was the song "Put It There, Pal", which became a Crosby-Hope theme classic. In the tune, the two entertainers deride each other about their recent flop films, Hope's *Let's Face It* and Crosby's *Dixie*. Although "Put It

There, Pal," with the contemporary references to their films, made no sense in this 1890s period piece, audiences by this time were coming to see the stars and forgave them any illogical departure from reality. In fact, by the time the fourth picture in the series appeared, most moviegoers were expecting the deviations.

But the set of *Utopia* was far from harmonic. Simply bringing the three stars together at the same time was proving hectic. All three had busy schedules and lucrative careers, and scheduling was difficult. When cameras on *Utopia* finally rolled, there was some discord among the famous threesome who had traveled those other successful roads together.

Some of that friction came to a head when, at one point in the filming, Hope and Crosby both wanted to play in a charity golf match and were apparently oblivious to the fact that they were scheduled to shoot a musical scene with Lamour. It was a scene that reportedly had been rescheduled from a previous Hope-Crosby truancy.

For this particular number in which Lamour sang "Personality," she had to be corseted and poured into a lovely evening gown. The elaborate hairstyles and makeup also took about two hours, so to be on the set by 9 A.M., she had to arrive at the studio by 6 A.M.

On the day of the shoot, Lamour got ready and arrived on the soundstage about 9 A.M., but Hope and Crosby were nowhere to be found. She and the rest of the players, extras, and crew waited. Most of that wasted time she spent leaning on a slant board provided for actresses with an outfit too tight for sitting. At the lunch break she got out of the gown and, though she objected loudly, agreed to get back into it for the presumed afternoon shooting.

At about 4 P.M., Gary Cooper wandered onto the stage and heard a furious Lamour sputtering about two inconsiderate actors. "You shouldn't let those guys take advantage of you," said Cooper. "Why don't you just give them a taste of their own medicine? Go back to your dressing room, take off your costume and makeup, and go home."

Although hesitant, she agreed, and left in a rage. No sooner had she gotten into her street clothes than the wandering duo arrived. When Paramount's production chief Buddy DeSylva called to find out why Lamour was not on the set, she told the Paramount executive exactly how she felt.

Fortunately, the next day all was patched up. Not surprisingly, Crosby and Hope took turns teasing Lamour, calling her "that temperamental Lamour woman who stormed off the set." But they never pulled another stunt like that again.

Another rather ugly scene occurred with a rather ugly extra—a full-grown grizzly bear.

In the scene, Hope and Crosby are bundled up under covers in their heavy winter coats sleeping on the floor of a cabin when the bear, who only moments before was released from his chain, walks in and starts sniffing around. The two stars had been told that after the director said "Cut!" they were not to move until the bear's trainer had the animal back on the chain and into the cage. The twosome did not realize how important that little fact was until after the scene was finished. During the scene, the bear walked over the lump consisting of Crosby and Hope and growled fiercely. Literally shaking beneath their covers, the two stars feared they might become the bear's dinner. After the director said "Cut!" and the trainer had said "O.K., I've got him back in the cage," Crosby got up and said, "Well, that's all with this thing. To hell with that!"

They had been lucky: the next day the bear mauled its trainer, reportedly tearing the man's arm off.

Still other mishaps occurred on the set of *Utopia*. Crosby and Hope were climbing up the side of a mountain set in the studio with Hope on top and Crosby on the bottom of the rope. The rope broke, and Hope fell back onto Crosby. "In those days, we were numbers one and two at the box office," Hope said later. "Paramount didn't care—I guess it was another way of dropping your option!"

In *Road to Utopia*, Hope successfully woos Lamour for the first time, but it was not originally written that way. The original ending for the film was a wild one, created by writers Panama and Frank. The way they wrote it, the dastardly villain ties Lamour to a log in a sawmill. Crosby and Hope arrive to save her from the approaching buzz saw, and they measure hands on an ax handle like a baseball bat to see which one will make the courageous rescue. The scene then fades out and fades in again years later. Crosby and Hope are walking in a garden with Lamour in the middle, and as they part, Crosby walks off with half of Lamour and Hope walks off with the other half.

"I think it's great!" said Buddy DeSylva, the head of production. But a few weeks later, he said, "I've got the finish." His idea had all three of the stars trying to escape the bad guys at the end of the picture. As they are chased out onto the frozen wasteland, a crack in the ice pack develops and separates Lamour and Hope on one side and Crosby and the villains on the other. Even though Lamour loves Crosby, Hope and Lamour get married because they assume Crosby has been killed.

Chester Hooton (Bob Hope), Sal (Dorothy Lamour), and Duke Johnson (Bing Crosby) are halted by murderers Sperry (Robert Barrat) and McGurk (Nestor Paiva) in the 1945 film *Road to Utopia*.

Years later, Lamour and Hope have long been married when Crosby pays them a visit. They introduce their son, who turns out to look exactly like Crosby. Hope shrugs his shoulders and says, "We adopted him."

Hope had some concerns about the ending as it was filmed. "But Buddy," he said to DeSylva at the time, "you'll never get past the censors."

"Just watch us," DeSylva said confidently. And he did.

After traveling four "Roads," almost every conceivable new gag and situation had been utilized. For the fifth "Road" film, it was back to the basics. The next film would bring the sojourners closer to the original concept of the first film, *Singapore*, and some of the "Road" films that followed—*Road to Rio* would be a comedy filled with music.

Road to Utopia
A Paramount Picture

Released: December 1945
Running time: 90 minutes

Producer Paul Jones; *Production Secretary* Marie Morris; *Director* Hal Walker; *1st Assistant Director* Alvin Ganzer; *2d Assistant Director* Joe Lefert; *2d Unit Director* Buddy Coleman; *1st Assistant Director, 2d Unit* Herb Coleman; *Co-Director, 2d Unit* C. Coleman; *Directorial Secretary* Ann Mack; *Original Screenplay by* Norman Panama and Melvin Frank; *Script Clerk* Laprele Jones; *Dialogue Coach* J. Vincent; *Animations* Jerry Fairbanks; *Director of Photography* Lionel Lindon; *Second Cameraman* Neal Beckner; *Camera Operator, 2d Unit* Ed Soderberg; *Camera Operator, 2d Unit* A. Langstrom Jones; *Assistant Cameraman* Jack Bishop; *Art Direction* Hans Dreier and Roland Anderson; *Transparency Supervisor* Farciot Edouart (assisted by Loyal Griggs); *Editorial Supervisor* Stuart Gilmore; *Special Effects Supervisor* Gordon Jennings, A.S.C. (assisted by Paul Lerpae); *Matte Paintings* Gordon Jennings (assisted by Jan Domela and Irmin Roberts); *Costumes* Edith Head; *Instructor or Coach* Francis Dawson; *Musical Numbers Conducted by* Robert Emmett Dolan; *Music Score* Leigh Harline; *Vocal Arrangements* Joseph J. Lilley; *Song Lyrics by* Johnny Burke; *Music by* James Van Heusen; *Sound Recording by* Hugo Grenzbach and Philip Wisdom; *Music Mixers* Joel Moss and Philip Wisdom; *Dance Supervisor* S. Ledner; *Dances Staged by* Danny Dare; *Dance Prop Man* Bob Goodstein; *Assistant Dance Director* Al Mann; *Dance Secretary* Nelle Armstrong; *Unit Manager* H. Schwartz; *Livestock* William Hurley; *Unit Manager, 2d Unit* Frank Kies; *Unit Manager, 2d Unit* N. Lacey; *Assistant Unit Manager, 2d Unit* Andy Durkas; *Property Man* T. Plews; *Set Dressing Supervisor* Sam Comer; *Miniatures* Gordon Jennings (assisted by Ivyl Burke and Devereux Jennings); *Makeup Supervision* Wally Westmore; *Hairdressing Supervisor* Leonora Sabine; *Set Decoration* George Sawley; *Location Auditor* Earl Livingstone; *2d Unit Script Clerk* Marvin Weldon; *2d Unit Wardrobe Man* Lew Brown.

CAST

Duke Johnson/Junior Hooton	Bing Crosby
Chester Hooton	Bob Hope
Sal (Val Hoyden)	Dorothy Lamour
Kate	Hillary Brooke
Ace Larson	Douglass Dumbrille
LeBec	Jack LaRue

Sperry	Robert Barrat
McGurk	Nestor Paiva
Narrator	Robert Benchley
Mr. Latimer	Will Wright
Ringleader of Henchmen	Jimmy Dundee
Newsboy	William Benedict
Husky Sailor	Art Foster
Purser	Arthur Loft
Husky Sailor	Sammy Stein
Newsboy	Gerald Pierce
Official at Boat	Stanley Andrews
Captain on Boat	Alan Bridge
1st Policeman	Lee Shumway
2d Policeman	Al Ferguson
Top Hat	Romaine Callender
Tough Ship's Purser	Paul Newlan
1st Man	Jack Rutherford
2d Man	Al Hill
Townsman	George Anderson
1st Official (Cop)	Edgar Dearing
2d Official (Cop)	Charles Wilson
Sailor	Frank Marlowe
Bit Man—Zambini's	Brandon Hurst
Bit Man—Zambini's	Don Gallaher
Bit Man—Zambini's	Bud Harrison
Master of Ceremonies	Edward Emerson
Hotel Manager	Ronnie Rondell
Henchmen	Allen Pomeroy
	Jack Stoney
Bit Waiter	George McKay
Bartender	Pat West
Bit Girl	Joyce Norman
Bartender	Frank Moran
Bartender	Bobby Barber
Bit Man	Al Murphy
Ring Leader	Larry Daniels
Bit Man	George McKay
Bear	Charles Gemora
Prospector	Charles Sullivan
Prospector	George Lloyd
Eskimo	Jimmy Lono
Girl	Claire James
Girl	Maxine Fife
Santa Claus	Ferdinand Munier
Bit Part	Carmelle Bergstrom
Man	Jimmy Dundee

Road to Rio,
1947

Many "Roads" had been traveled by the three intrepid adventurers by the time 1947 rolled around, and some people thought the series had gotten away from its musical roots. Some critics, as well as patrons, said the films had started to rely too heavily on comedy and did not have enough music.

But that changed in *Road to Rio,* probably the most musical of all the "Road" films. The clever comedy was still a dominant feature of the film, but there was also an ample supply of musical numbers with Crosby's big ballads, the Crosby-Hope patter duets, and Lamour's sexy solos. And if that were not enough, the *Road to Rio* added the popular Andrews Sisters and Wiere Brothers to the successful formula.

Like David Butler and Hal Walker, director Norman Z. McLeod had a background in comedy, and his career in film directing continued along that course. That is probably why his deft directing helped make *Road to Rio* one of the funniest, and most musical, films in the series.

McLeod was a writer and gagman early in his show business career but turned to directing in 1928. He directed a few films for Fox and Hal Roach, but almost all of his films were for Paramount. After directing Hope and Crosby in *Rio* in 1947, McLeod went on to direct Hope in several other films, including *The Paleface* (1948), *My Favorite Spy* (1951), *Casanova's Big Night* (1954), and *Alias Jesse James* (1959).

McLeod gained some of his early experience in comedy by directing the nonsensical Marx Brothers in two films, *Monkey Business* (1931) and *Horse Feathers* (1932). Although not as zany as the brothers, Hope and Crosby had their crazy moments.

Bob Hope laughs it up with two of the Wiere Brothers on the set of *Road to Rio* (1947).

When McLeod took over the directing reins for *Rio*, however, he announced he would be keeping an eye on the pair's propensity to "introduce gags about themselves and Hollywood." McLeod's intentions came to naught, however.

Unlike a boisterous David Butler, Mcleod was a quiet and tranquil director, rarely yelling at anyone. Crosby and Hope eventually started calling him the Mumbler, often asking him to speak up so they could hear his directions.

What McLeod brought to the renowned "Road" series was a sense of its original melodious flair. By incorporating musical acts such as the Andrews Sisters and the Wiere Brothers, complete with specialty numbers, *Rio* was the most musical "Road" picture since *Singapore*. And, surprisingly, the comedy was not lost in the process.

The musical influence was also evident in the story line. Hope and Crosby play musicians in the film, allowing for numerous musical interludes, some of which even forwarded the plot. Hope, as "Hot Lips" Barton, a trumpet player, and Crosby, as clarinetist Scat Sweeney, perform some musical bits. In one scene, they don black tuxedos and bow ties to work as extras in a movie as part of a dance band. Later in *Rio* they play in the ship's band, working for their passage across the ocean. Then, once they are in Rio, they form their own band.

But the return to a more musical nature was not the only factor that was different about this fifth "Road" picture. The changes behind the cameras were even more obvious. This time around, Hope and Crosby each financed a third of the film while Paramount financed the final third, enabling the two stars to have more decision-making control. This made for some interesting encounters among the three stars and some different reactions by two-thirds of the financial team, namely Hope and Crosby.

On the first four "Road" pictures, Hope and Crosby sometimes gave the production staff a difficult task. As soon as a director called "Cut! Lunch!" Crosby and Hope would take off. Hope, with his writers or business associates, usually headed to a restaurant for lunch, while Crosby, more often than not, would cut out for a driving range or golf course to hit a bucket of golf balls or play a few holes.

After the one-hour lunch break, the director would say, "Round 'em up" and the poor assistant director was forced to pick up a phone and start coaxing the crooner and the comedian back to the soundstage. If Hope happened to be in the middle of a radio script or Crosby was hitting his nine-iron really well, it could take some time. After a while, the assistant directors would start calling the twosome 15 minutes before they were really needed, but even that trick did not always work.

But all that changed when the two stars became part owners of the *Road to Rio*. Throughout the filming, Crosby and Hope hardly left the set. The minute that the hour allotted for lunch had passed, Crosby might say, "All right, let's get moving. What are we waiting for?" Hope might add, "Let's start shooting. Come on, we're wasting time." Their tendency to have friends and relatives visit them on the sets of the "Road" films also was curbed during the filming of *Road to Rio*.

At one point in the production schedule, a carnival scene was being filmed and the stage was jammed with extras. Because of the large crowd, the crew was taking quite some time to light the set. After a substantial delay, Hope finally asked what was taking so long.

"It's a big scene," said director Norman Z. McLeod. "It takes time to light."

At last the scene was lit, and over the loudspeaker McLeod said, "All right, this will be a take. Will the visitors please step back."

At that moment, hundreds of people retreated from the set. "My God," said one of the crew members, "We lighted all those visitors. I thought they were extras!"

At first, Crosby and Hope complained about the delay, but quickly abandoned their objection when it was pointed out that about 300 of the visitors were the stars' friends or relatives.

The roles of part owners of the film also had Hope and Crosby checking other items a little more closely. One day Hope teased Lamour about the low cut of her gown designed by Edith Head and embarrassed her during the first take of a scene. After Lamour muffed her lines a few times, she yelled, "Stop everything until Mr. Hope has had a good look."

Hope took a long look at the dress and called Crosby over.

"How much do you think this dress cost, partner?" he asked the crooner.

"Somewhere around $4,000," Lamour chimed in.

"Well," Hope said, after he and Crosby recovered from the shock, "we'll rent it out to at least six more gals before we're through with it."

If becoming part owners of the *Road to Rio* was not enough, Hope and Crosby were partners in other business ventures as well. At about the time filming began on *Rio*, they found what they thought was a promising investment, a soft drink called Lime Cola, and put some money into the enterprise. A promoter had convinced them to invest about $25,000 apiece with the promise that he was going to put Coca-Cola out of business.

The thought occurred to the two business tycoons: Why not use *Road to Rio* to help sell Lime Cola? They mulled it over and decided to have a large sign promoting the drink displayed prominently in one of the scenes of the film. Although it is commonplace today, plugging commercial products in movies was unheard of in the mid-forties, and the Paramount brass objected.

"You can't do that," argued a Paramount attorney. "That's advertising."

"We can't do that, huh?" Hope said. "Say, Bing—who owns this picture?"

"Why you own a third, and I own a third," Crosby replied.

"Let's see—one third and one third makes two thirds, right? I guess Paramount is outvoted."

The Lime Cola ad remained in the *Road to Rio,* but Lime Cola did not put Coca-Cola out of business. Instead, Lime Cola went down the drain, and the duo's money was never recovered.

Even though they were businessmen regarding the film's production, Crosby and Hope were still like little kids on the set. It got so silly that they could not even move from their dressing rooms to the set first thing in the morning without clowning.

In those days Paramount supplied their stars with bicycles for transport around the lot. Hope and Crosby used them to good effect to see who could arrive on the set last in order to "make an entrance." The scenario would go something like this: Since neither wanted to get there first, each would devise plans to allow the other to arrive ahead of him. If Crosby started out on his bicycle, for example, he would not go directly to the set, but instead would travel around the lot a bit and would return the back way to his dressing room to watch for Hope. Then Hope, having seen Crosby leave his dressing room earlier, would start off, figuring Crosby was already on the set. Hope would walk into the studio and say, "Where's the Groaner? Where's Fatso?" but Crosby was still back in his dressing room.

But the clowning and practical jokes were not limited to just Crosby and Hope. Often the two stars would engage in some festive good humor with Paramount executives, most notably Buddy DeSylva. "We used to really fix DeSylva up at the rushes," said Crosby.

DeSylva and other executives would look at the results of the previous day's shooting, and there were almost always a couple of scenes with special material. "They had no idea what was coming," said Crosby. "We'd put in something very dirty and they'd come rushing out of the projection room and send us notes which we'd ignore. We'd let them believe we were going to use the scenes and that we were going to fight for them. Then they began to realize that it was all just a gag."

But there were still plenty of gags on film too. Despite the more musical nature of *Road to Rio,* it was filled with the typical Hope-Crosby antics.

In the film, Scat Sweeney (Crosby) and "Hot Lips" Barton (Hope) are a pair of broke musicians from Hollywood. They play a one-night stand at a carnival, burn the place down (a plot element borrowed from *Road to Zanzibar*) then stow away on a liner for Rio de Janeiro.

On board, Crosby and Hope encounter Lucia Maria de Andrade (Lamour), whose sinister aunt (splendidly portrayed by Gale Sondergaard) is marrying her off to a disreputable character in order to gain control of the family fortune. Crosby and Hope discover the aunt is hypnotizing Lamour, but not before Lamour turns them in as stowaways. They patty-cake their way out of the jam but run into Sondergaard's henchmen (from whom they have stolen some suits) and then obligingly go into the ship captain's custody. Lamour later vouches for them, and the captain offers the two musicians a spot in the band to work their passage to Rio. (They later use the patty-cake routine on the crooks, hypnotizing them to do it to each other as Hope says: "That's what they get for not seeing our pictures.")

The two musicians make it to Rio, and Crosby smuggles Lamour off the ship and past her aunt in a bull fiddle case, unbeknownst to Hope, who is against getting mixed up with Lamour. On the gangplank, as Hope and Crosby carry the Lamour-laden bull fiddle case off the ship, Crosby whispers to the case, "Can you breathe all right?" Hope, thinking Crosby is talking to him, says: "Sure, I can breathe." Then he sniffs the air. "See!"

More clever dialogue ensues when they arrive at the luxurious suite at the hotel with Lamour still in the case. Crosby again addresses Lamour as she gets out of the case.

> Crosby: "You all right?"
> Hope: "You keep askin' me—I'm all right! I'm all right!"
> Crosby: (this time addressing Hope) "O.K. then. Put this over in the corner, will ya?"
> Hope obligingly pulls the now empty bull fiddle case to the corner of the lavish room as Crosby addresses Lamour.
> Crosby: "You're not a little stiff, are ya?"
> Hope (still unaware of Lamour's presence): "Stiff! I haven't had a drink since I got off the boat."

In Rio, Crosby hires three natives (the Wiere Brothers—guitar, flute, and violin) and teaches them jive talk. This results in another witty and clever bit of business.

Variety noted that "Norman Z. McLeod's direction blends the music and comedy into fast action and sock chuckles," but *Road to Rio* writers Edmund Beloin and Jack Rose gave McLeod a good script with which to work.

Edmund Beloin later scripted *A Connecticut Yankee in King Arthur's Court* (1949), in which Crosby starred, and he also wrote screenplays for lighthearted films featuring Jerry Lewis (after his split with Dean Martin) and Elvis Presley. Beloin also teamed up with Rose to write Hope's *My Favorite Brunette* in 1947, the same year they filmed *Road to Rio*.

Jack Rose, in addition to working with Beloin, had a number of writing credits to his name, including films for Jerry Lewis and Dean Martin (after their split) and Hope's *The Seven Little Foys* (1955) and *Beau James* (1957), which he cowrote with Melville Shavelson. Rose later produced a number of comedies for Paramount, including Cary Grant's *Houseboat* (1958), Danny Kaye's *On the Double* (1961), and Dean Martin's *Who's Been Sleeping in My Bed?* (1964). Rose, with his future partner Mel Shavelson, developed and wrote Danny Thomas's long-running television series *Make Room for Daddy*.

As in all the "Road" films, *Rio* possesses a good portion of crazy adventures which are adapted nicely to the exotic atmosphere of the South American city. The opulent wedding scene toward the end of the film features a funny musical routine with Crosby outfitted in gypsylike garb, complete with a pencil-thin mustache and an earring. Hope, with a flowery, flowing skirt and checkered blouse, is dressed as a Carmen Miranda character, including a headdress of assorted fruits. It is an obvious takeoff of the standard dance spectaculars which highlighted many Latin American–type Hollywood musicals.

Eventually, Hope and Crosby save Lamour from her evil aunt by getting the "papers," which reveal to the appropriate authorities that the whole marriage was a crooked deal. (The audience, however, never finds out what the "papers" say. The writers provide themselves an easy out when Hope asks Crosby what information the "papers" contain and Crosby responds: "The world must never know.")

Once again several popular songs came out of a "Road" film via the collaboration of Johnny Burke and Jimmy Van Heusen. The Crosby ballad "But Beautiful" is among his hits. Other catchy tunes included "You Don't Have to Know the Language," in which the Andrews Sisters added their voices to Crosby's. Other songs in *Road to Rio* included "For What?" by the Andrews Sisters, Hope and Crosby's "Apalachicola, Fla." and Lamour's "Experience."

Aside from being one of the better "Road" pictures, *Road to Rio* featured an actress who was a part of history. Gale Sondergaard, who played Lamour's aunt in the film, is one of the most distinguished

"Hot Lips" Barton (Bob Hope) and Scat Sweeney (Bing Crosby) perform "Apalachicola, Fla." the opening song in the movie *Road to Rio* (1947).

actresses of all the professionals in the "Road" series. She was the winner of the first Best Supporting Actress Oscar in 1936 for her role as Faith in *Anthony Adverse*. It was also her first movie.

In addition to *Rio*, Sondergaard appeared in *The Cat and the Canary* (1939) with Hope, *The Mark of Zorro* (1940), *My Favorite Blonde* (1942) with Hope, and *A Night to Remember* (1943). She was also Basil Rathbone's deadly opponent in *Sherlock Holmes and the Spider Woman* (1944).

Frank Faylen did not gain much fame from his appearance in *Rio*, but he was a part of some other great films including *The Grapes of*

Wrath (1940), *Gunfight at the O.K. Corral* (1957), and *North to Alaska* (1960). He also played Ernie, the cab driver in *It's a Wonderful Life* (1946), and Bim, the sanitarium orderly in the Ray Milland classic *The Lost Weekend* (1945). Still, his claim to fame may have come later in life when he was a regular on the *Dobie Gillis* television show as Dobie's father, Herbert T. Gillis.

Jerry Colonna made a brief appearance in *Rio* when, at the end of the movie, he leads a band of cavalry to the rescue, but they never quite arrive.

Rio was the first "Road" to make use of guest stars—the Andrews Sisters (Patti, Maxene, and LaVerne) and the Wiere Brothers (Harry, Herbert, and Sylvester)—who set the stage, somewhat, for the cameo appearances of other stars in the final two "Road" films, *Bali* and *Hong Kong*.

The Andrews Sisters, who had been more familiar to moviegoers in "B" pictures, were given the role in *Rio* as a result of their association with Crosby on records. The Andrews Sisters were featured in several Abbott and Costello films, such as *Buck Privates* and *Hold That Ghost* (both in 1941). The Wiere Brothers appeared in *The Great American Broadcast* (1941).

Other actors and actresses who appeared in the *Road to Rio* include Joseph Vitale, Frank Puglia, Nestor Paiva (who also appeared in *Road to Morocco* and *Road to Utopia*), and Robert Barrat (who also appeared in *Utopia*).

In *Rio*, Hope again wins Lamour's hand in marriage (as he did in *Utopia*), but this time it is done via subterfuge.

Throughout the film, Sondergaard uses hypnosis on Lamour, and Hope uses the same approach to win Lamour's love. A bewildered Crosby learns later how Hope got the girl when he trails the happy couple to Niagara Falls, where they are spending their honeymoon. Peering through a keyhole, Crosby sees Hope dangling a gleaming pendant before Lamour's eyes, casting her under a hypnotic spell.

The hypnosis bit also caused some laughs when the cameras were not rolling.

Lamour, supposedly hypnotized by Sondergaard off and on throughout the film, would change her mood on screen as she was given different orders. For example, in a nightclub dressing room scene, Lamour walks up to Crosby and says, "I hate you. I loathe you. I despise you," and then whacks him right across the face.

"But, baby," Crosby interjects.

Scat Sweeney (Bing Crosby) persuades a hesitant "Hot Lips" Barton (Bob Hope) to perform a high-wire act in the 1947 film *Road to Rio*.

"That sounds like Bogey," Hope quips, and then Lamour turns to him with a right to the jaw.

"This dame is slap-happy!" Hope yells out.

"Cut!" called director Norman Z. McLeod. "Let's try that again!"

After the scene, Hope went over to Lamour and, rubbing his jaw, said, "Look, Dottie, the sound department can put in the loud smack. So you know you don't really have to hit me that hard."

"Yeah," agreed Crosby, "or else you'll be known as Rocky Graziano Lamour."

Road to Rio was probably the best-structured film of the series. It had a more intelligible plot than some of the other "Road" films, and the leads could conceivably have been played by other talented actors and actresses, although probably not with the same degree of success.

As musical as *Rio* was, some of the famous "Road" bits were still a part of the chemistry. References outside the plot appear in the film almost from the beginning. In one of the early scenes, Hope is in a sparse hotel room with his feet up on a desk playing the trumpet with "Thanks for the Memory" (his theme song) wafting through the air. A short time later, Hope, clothed in sequin-studded tights and jersey, is hanging on a carnival tightrope calling for help. He pauses and calmly says, "You know this picture could end right here."

The dialogue in *Rio* was witty and seemingly spontaneous. At one point early in the film, Hope, disguised as a slab of beef in a sack hung in the ship's meat locker, is finally rescued by Crosby. As Crosby searches the dozens of slabs of meat hung on the racks, he cuts one can-vas bag open which contains pig meat. "Well, I'm getting warm," Crosby announces proudly. "That's ham."

Special effects played less of a part in *Rio* than in some previous films, but they were not discarded entirely. At one point Hope's trum-pet falls into a bucket of soap suds, and he winds up blowing soap bub-bles through the instrument.

But the one-liners still stole the show.

Throughout the film Lamour is hypnotized into strange behav-ior by Sondergaard and states, "I find myself saying things and I don't know why I say them."

"Why don't you just run for Congress and forget about us?" says the exasperated Hope.

The finale of *Road to Rio* is frantic and funny, with shots of Jerry Colonna, adorned in a printed shirt, black vest, and readied sword, leading about 30 Brazilian cavalry men to the rescue, but they never arrive. "What do you know, we never quite made it," Colonna shrugs. "Exciting, though, wasn't it?"

By this time, the "Road" series and the three stars were at the height of their popularity. Others in the movie-making industry took advantage of the series' success with their own humorous lines.

During the filming of *Rio*, guest June Haver commented on Hope's radio show that she was going to star in *Scudda-Hoo! Scudda-Hey!*

a story about two mules. "Why," Hope asked, "is Twentieth Century Fox starring such a beautiful girl like you with two jackasses?"

"I don't know," she replied, "but it didn't hurt Dorothy Lamour at Paramount."

By this time, five "Roads" and seven years had been covered by Crosby, Hope, and Lamour, and it almost appeared as if there was not much new they could add to the act. So rather than tampering with a good thing as far as the performances were concerned, they went a different route and altered some things on the technical side of movie making for their next picture.

Road to Rio
A Paramount Picture

Released: December 1947
Running time: 100 minutes

Producer Daniel Dare; *Director* Norman Z. McLeod; *Assistant Director* Oscar Rudolph; *Original Story and Screenplay by* Edmund Beloin and Jack Rose; *Editor* Ellsworth Hoagland; *Director of Photography* Ernest Laszlo; *Art Direction* Hans Dreier and Earl Hedrick; *Special Photographic Effects* Gordon Jennings and Paul Lerpae; *Process Photography* Farciot Edouart; *Costumes* Edith Head; *Musical Director* Robert Emmett Dolan; *Vocal Arrangements* Joseph J. Lilley; *Music Associate* Troy Sanders; *New Song Lyrics by* Johnny Burke; *Music by* James Van Heusen; *Sound Recording* Harold Lewis and Walter Oberst; *Dances Staged by* Bernard Pearce and Billy Daniels; *Makeup Supervisor* Wally Westmore; *Set Decoration* Sam Comer and Ray Moyer.

CAST

Scat Sweeney	Bing Crosby
"Hot Lips" Barton	Bob Hope
Lucia Maria De Andrade	Dorothy Lamour
Catherine Vail	Gale Sondergaard
Trigger	Frank Faylen
Tony	Joseph Vitale
Rodrigues	Frank Puglia
Cardoso	Nestor Paiva
Johnson	Robert Barrat

The Stone-Barton Puppeteers	Themselves
The Carioca Boys	Themselves
Cavalry Captain	Jerry Colonna
Three Musicians	The Wiere Brothers
The Andrews Sisters	Themselves
Sherman Malloy	George Meeker
Captain Harmon	Stanley Andrews
Ship's Purser	Harry Woods
Samson	Tor Johnson
Specialty Dancer	Albert Ruiz
Specialty Dancer	Laura Corbay
Steward	Donald Kerr
Assistant Purser	Stanley Blystone
The Prefeito	George Sorel
Dancer	John "Skins" Miller
Roustabout	Frank Hagney
Roustabout	Duke York
Roustabout	Ralph Gomez
Stampman	William Newell
Stevedore	Fred Zender
Ship's Officer	Alan Bridge
Foreman	Ralph Dunn
Bit Man	Charles Cooley
1st Butcher	Paul Newlan
2d Butcher	George Lloyd
Valet	George Chandler
2d Stampman	John Mallon
Assistant Purser	Pat Lane
Steward	Jack Gargan
Barber	Gino Corrado
Passenger	Norma Gentner
Mr. Stanton	Arthur Q. Bryan
Bit Woman	Babe London
Bit Man	Hal K. Dawson
Bellhop	Rolando Barrera
Bellhop	Lionel Dante
Waiter	Stenio Ozorio
Entertainer	Marquita Rivera
Bit Girl	Jeanne Gail
Brazilian Manservent	Julian Rivero
Charwoman	Patsy O'Byrne
Pretty Girl	Lucille Barkley
Flower Girl	Robbie Franks
Maitre D'	Don Avalier
Maitre D'	Rene Dussaq
Spectator	Kathyrine Valk
Maitre D'	John Mallon

Airline Hostess	Barbara Pratt
Brazilian Pilot	Victor Romito
Pilot	Tad Van Brunt
Girl	Kathy Young
Cavalry Officer	Raul Roulien
Specialty Dancer	Rudolfo Silva
Specialty Dancer	Jane Everett
Specialty Dancer	Rudolpho Andrian
Specialty Dancer	Bonnie Vallarino
Photo Double and Specialty Dancer	Tom Ladd
Photo Double and Specialty Dancer	Byron Poindexter
Peasant	Delmar Costello
Aristocratic Brazilian	Dolores Castle
Wedding Guest	Joe Whitehead
Dignified Gentleman	Pepito Perez
Peasant	Arthur Vallee
Cowhand	Frank Ferguson
Farmer	Charles Middleton
Buck	Ray Teal
Hula Dancer	Norma Gentner
Barker	Brandon Hurst
Carnival Girl	Llorna Jordan
Strong Man	Freddie Zender
Barker	Frederic Nay
Pretty Girl	Renee Randall
Barker	John Mallon
Barker	Tom Dugan
Barker	Bert Hanlon

Road to Bali, 1952

Bing Crosby, Bob Hope, and Dorothy Lamour had played some colorful characters in the first five "Road" pictures, but moviegoers were robbed of the full effect by limited technology.

The biggest news attached to the sixth "Road" picture was that it would be made in glorious Technicolor. That particular cinematic aspect added greatly to the motion picture, giving many scenes an exotic element that had been difficult to capture on black and white film. But making the movie in color also had some influence on costumes and the story line.

At one point in the production, someone suggested that Hope and Crosby do a bagpipe routine. There had also been a proposal that Lamour be called Princess MacTavish in the film. The reasoning behind all this Scottish proclivity was very simple—they had already decided to make one of Lamour's sarongs out of authentic Scotch plaid, and of the several tartans they screen-tested, the MacTavish plaid turned out best in Technicolor. (In the finished product, however, Lamour was named Princess Lalah.)

The plot of *Bali* is similar to those of all the other "Road" films. Vaudevillians Harold Gridley (Hope) and George Cochran (Crosby) are forced to leave Australia because of a pair of matrimony-minded girls. Their voyage takes them to a South Sea island where they meet a princess (Lamour) who is searching for sunken treasure which rightfully belongs to her but is also being sought by the villainous Ken Arok (Murvyn Vye). Hope and Crosby encounter headhunters, wild animals, volcanoes, and a giant squid along the way. Also featured in the film are Peter Coe, Ralph Moody, and Leon Askin.

Although the picture was popular with audiences, *Variety* gave it a lukewarm review, saying: "There's no story to speak of in the script … but the framework is there on which to hang a succession of amusing quips and physical comedy dealing with romantic rivalry and chuckle competition between the two leads."

Frank Butler was back to write *Road to Bali* for Hope and Crosby but collaborated with Hal Kanter and William Morrow. Both Kanter and Morrow are probably better known for their work in later movies, especially for the musical flicks of Elvis Presley and Martin and Lewis when they were still performing as a film team.

Morrow, Edmund Beloin, and two other scribes wrote a 1940 film for Jack Benny and Fred Allen called *Love Thy Neighbor*. Interestingly enough, Allen and Benny carried on a long, carefully sustained feud from their radio days, much like that of Hope and Crosby.

In *Road to Bali* the Johnny Burke and James Van Heusen songwriting collaboration turned out Lamour's "Moonflower" and the delightful "The Merry-Go-Runaround" performed by the three stars. Other Burke/Van Heusen songs included Crosby's "To See You (Is to Love You)," Hope and Crosby's "Chicago Style," and the comic and the crooner's "Hoot Man."

As with the other films, *Bali* was little more than a vehicle for Bing Crosby and Bob Hope to indulge in their comical escapades. The movie was filled with personal references and subtle insults, much to the pleasure of audiences and critics alike. For example, the mutual distrust of their characters is restated in an opening scene. Crosby and Hope are singing and dancing to "Chicago Style," and as they sway right and left together at center stage, Crosby promises Hope: "Wait'll you see what I got lined up for you, boy!"

"What is it? A dame?" asks the interested Hope.

"What else would I line up for you," says Crosby casually.

Asks Hope: "What's wrong with her?"

Although special effects and references outside the plot were not as prevalent in *Bali* as in some other films, they were still a "Road" trademark. One classic scene in *Road to Bali* has Hope and Crosby in the midst of a jungle watching Dorothy Lamour swim. The two are attired in their casual sport shirts, slacks, and sailor caps and are leaning on a branch that is about waist high. Trees and other foliage surround them, and the water is just below their outstretched bodies. The branch suddenly breaks away, but the two stars remain in their leaning positions. Crosby asks Hope: "Why don't we fall?" Hope deadpans,

"Paramount wouldn't dare, at your age." These lines and the special effects used in the scene were prime "Road" material.

Another reference outside the plot appears in a scene in which Hope and Crosby, fresh on the lam from two girls with marriage on their minds, are making their way through a herd of sheep in a meadow. They start singing "The Whiffenpoof Song," and the little lambs accompany them in the chorus with "Baa ... Baa ... Baa," to which Crosby says, "Fred Waring must have played through here."

Still another reference not related to the plot has Hope and Crosby surrounded by half a dozen scantily clad native women when an agonized scream is heard offscreen. "What was that?" asks Crosby. "Errol Flynn," Hope explains. "He can't stand it."

Later, Lamour asks the two men if they always fight over women. "What else can we fight over," says Hope, "we never had any money." Then he looks into the camera and explains for his fellow millionaire: "That's for Washington."

Another "Road" fixture appeared again in *Bali*—the patty-cake routine. This time around the comedian and the singer are imprisoned in a stone and bamboo jail cell and pull the bit on two natives who have captured them. The astute natives, however, duck out of the way as Hope and Crosby deliver the blows. The two stars knock each other out as the natives simply exit the dungeon.

Throughout their careers, the simulated Hope-Crosby feud focused on Hope's envy of Crosby's singing ability. The lines in *Road to Bali* were just another opportunity to fan the vendetta flame. In one scene Crosby and Hope sit at a table in the galley of a ship dividing up the trinkets and baubles they have recovered in the sunken treasure. Crosby starts to go topside and a strain of music is heard. Hope looks around and then deadpans to the camera, "He's gonna sing, folks—now's the time to go out and get the popcorn."

Another bit in which the audience is part of the action has the two stars topside on the boat, with Hope explaining to Crosby how he got out of the diving suit when it appeared that the giant squid had him in its grasp.

In the film Hope leaps into the ocean in a diving suit pursuing sunken treasure and comes face to tentacle with a giant squid. To save Hope, Crosby and Lamour inflate Hope's diving suit from a shipboard pump, and the suit pops to the surface. After Crosby and Lamour get the puffed-up diving outfit back on board ship, the villains fire several bullets into the suit, but Hope is not inside. Moments later he crawls into the boat, a little tattered, but still alive.

George Cochran (Bing Crosby) and Harold Gridley (Bob Hope) each try to convince Lalah (Dorothy Lamour) that he is the right man for her in the *Road to Bali* (1952).

"How did you get out of that suit?" Crosby asks Hope moments later.

"Out of the diving suit?" queries Hope.

"Yeah."

"Well, it was easy. You see I was down at the bottom ..." and then he stops and, realizing that the audience is watching, takes Crosby upstage, out of earshot of the camera. Hope then exuberantly pantomimes the vicious fight he had with the sea monster on the ocean floor. When the discussion is over, Crosby walks back to the camera as if to speak, but simply shrugs, and walks out of the scene as the film continues.

With not too much concern for the plot, it was easy to work a number of stars into *Road to Bali* cameo roles. This was a slightly new departure for the series. In *Road to Rio* they used stars in guest spots (the Andrews Sisters, the Wiere Brothers, and Jerry Colonna), but *Bali* was the first time the series utilized cameo appearances—stars who appeared briefly in just one scene. It would be done again in *The Road to Hong Kong.*

Dean Martin and Jerry Lewis had one cameo spot in the film, as did Jane Russell. Russell appears in a cameo at the end of the picture as an exotic creature being coaxed from a straw basket via the melodic strains of a magical flute Hope has mastered. Earlier in the film, Hope lured ladies from a woven basket via his pied-piping, but at the end of the film, Russell, in a sexy red and black outfit with wide-brimmed hat, appears out of a basket and goes off with Crosby, who already has Lamour. "Hey, wait a minute. What are you going to do with two girls?" whines Hope as he is left alone on the sandy shore.

"That's my problem," said Crosby, as he wanders off into the sunset arm-in-arm with the two women.

That sets the stage for Hope's useless attempts to prevent the conclusion of the film. "This picture isn't over yet," pleads Hope, as he struggles to keep THE END from appearing on the screen. "Call the producers ... Call the writers ..."

Jane Russell, who tantalized moviegoers with her appearance in Howard Hughes's *The Outlaw* (1943), also appeared with Hope in *The Paleface* (1948) and *Son of Paleface* (1952). She also was teamed with Marilyn Monroe in *Gentlemen Prefer Blondes* (1953).

The inside jokes that kidded the movie-making industry in *Bali* were ingenious and plentiful. Humphrey Bogart had just won the Academy Award for best actor in *The African Queen* and in *Bali* he is shown in a cameo hauling a boat through a swamp, just as he did as the lead character in the most dramatic scene in *Queen*.

Another gag involving Bogart comes when he forgets his Oscar on the bank of the river. Crosby picks it up, and Hope snatches it away, saying, "Give me that—you've already got one." (Crosby had won the Oscar in 1946 for his performance as a priest in *Going My Way*.)

In still another cameo appearance in the film, Crosby's brother Bob, a band leader in his own right, comes into a scene in a khaki-colored hunting outfit, complete with pith helmet. Bob Crosby shoots his rifle into the air, and as he exits, Lamour asks Bing Crosby who the guy was. "That was my brother," Bing answers. "I promised him a shot in the picture."

Bob Crosby was an orchestra leader and actor who usually appeared onscreen with his Bob Cats and Dixieland Jazz Band. They performed in such films as *Presenting Lily Mars* (1943), *Thousands Cheer* (1943), and *Pardon My Rhythm* (1944).

Another scene on the beach has Hope finding a bottle washed ashore with a note in it.

"Return this bottle to Sam's Supermarket for 3-cent deposit," Hope reads.

"Isn't it a pity," said Crosby. "Every movie's got to have a message."

Still other lines in the film were definitive "Road" passages. At one point, Hope and Crosby are being carted off by headhunting savages when a young native boy approaches and touches Hope on the arm. The boy's mother comes up and drags the youngster away, saying: "How many times have I told you—don't play with your food."

In another scene, a threatening gorilla takes Hope in its arms and Crosby advises Hope to "Keep cool."

"Keep cool," Hope replies. "I'm numb."

Still another scene has Hope, Crosby, and Lamour sleeping in a bamboo hut in the jungle, and when Hope wakes up, he finds that Lamour is gone.

> Hope: "Hey, get up, she's not here. Lalah's gone."
> Crosby: "Maybe some dirty rat kidnapped her."
> Hope: "Oh, couldn't be, we're both here."

But, as always, the hijinks were not limited to the screen. Both Crosby and Hope celebrated birthdays while making *Bali* and the frivolity continued during breaks in the filming.

When Crosby celebrated his 51 years, protesting that he was "really only 48," Hope and Lamour presented him with a cake, and only one candle. "To save your embarrassment" read the inscription.

Hope's 49 years were marked by an old-fashioned rocking chair from Crosby and Lamour and a specially printed gag edition of the show business bible *Variety*. "Crosby Breaks in New Boy" screamed the mock headline. "Entertainment King Auditions New Stooge Replacement," said a subhead. Underneath both headlines was a large picture of Crosby with Jerry Lewis.

Other offscreen hilarity occurred when certain scenes did not seem to play exactly as director Hal Walker had in mind. During the filming of one scene, Crosby and Lamour are putting Hope in a diver's suit so he can search the bottom of the ocean to retrieve the sunken treasure. Lamour was supposed to open the door in Hope's oversized diving helmet and give him a kiss for luck. After trying it twice, she simply gave up and mildly protested to Walker.

"This window is too small," said Lamour. "I can't reach Bob's mouth."

"Turn in your sarong and get out!" Hope shouted in mock displeasure. "We should have hired a Ubangi for this part!"

Hope is eventually lowered into the water, and after a pause, Crosby calls to him over the intercom. "Have you found any treasure?"

"No," ad-libbed Hope, "but I just tripped over your money belt down here." These lines never made it to the final version of the picture.

In another scene, both Hope and Crosby are fumbling with their lines. "Better warm up Martin and Lewis," Lamour said to Walker, who had directed the other comedy team in several pictures. "They're not only funnier, but younger."

Everybody laughed except Hope and Crosby. "*You'd* better be careful how you talk to us," said Hope. "You can always be replaced by an actress."

In terms of directing, Walker added little to the series' success because by this time in the series, the characters were already well defined and the humor well established.

Bali was one of three films that the two stars owned a percentage of—the other two were *Rio* and *Hong Kong*. Aside from the profits that the arrangement would bring, owning a piece of the picture had other advantages.

In *Bali* there were several beach scenes for which tons of beautiful white sand were hauled in from Pebble Beach. Hope had just installed a one-hole golf course at his home, which included four bunkers without sand. Seeing all the sand around him on the set, he thought a deal could be arranged. He checked with Crosby and confirmed that the two of them did, indeed, own two-thirds of the sand used in the film. Crosby had no problem with Hope taking some of the sand for his course at home, but Hope ran into opposition when he asked the prop man to deliver the white stuff to his house.

"Take ten truckloads of this sand out to my house when we're done with it," Hope told the prop man.

"No dice," said the studio employee. "This is Paramount's sand."

Crosby and Hope had a little talk with the boys in the front office, and as a result, part of the *Road to Bali* is in Hope's backyard.

The five-year layoff after *Road to Rio* had not dampened the youthful exuberance of the team, and the formula for the "Road" films was still working. At its premiere, the *Road to Bali* was described as "a pantomime for grown-ups," and the film delighted moviegoers.

The threesome had now completed six "Roads" together and would not do it again for another ten years. The final "Road" they ambled down, however, was a bit rocky, in more ways than one.

Road to Bali
A Paramount Picture

Released: November 1952
Running time: 91 minutes

Producer Harry Tugend; *Production Secretary* Dorothy Smith; *Director* Hal Walker; *Assistant Director* John Coonan; *Assistant Directors* Rusty Meek, Bud Brill, and C. Jones; *Screenplay by* Frank Butler, Hal Kanter, and William Morrow; *Story by* Frank Butler and Harry Tugend; *Script Supervisor* Lupe Hall; *Dialogue Coach* Len Hendry; *Color by* Technicolor; *Director of Photography* George Barnes; *Technicolor Color Consultant* Monroe W. Burbank; *Art Direction* Hal Pereira and Joseph McMillan Johnson; *Special Photographic Effects* Gordon Jennings and Paul Lerpae; *Process Photography* Farciot Edouart; *Edited by* Archie Marshek; *2d Unit Cameraman* Duke Green; *1st Cameramen, 2d Unit* Harry Wilde and Wally Kelly; *Assistant Cameraman, 2d Unit* E. Wahrmann; *Underwater Test Camera* Lionel Lindon; *Prop Maker, 2d Unit* Eddie Sutherland; *Technical Assistant Cameraman* George Dye; *Costumes* Edith Head; *Wardrobe Woman* Ruth Davis Stella; *Sound Recording* Gene Merritt and John Cope; *Sound Recorder* Julia Miller; *Musical Director* Joseph J. Lilley; *Special Orchestral Arrangements* Van Cleave; *New Songs Lyrics by* Johnny Burke; *Music by* James Van Heusen; *Music Adviser* Troy Sanders; *Dance Director* Charles O'Curran; *Music and Dance Coordinator* S. Ledner; *Set Decoration* Sam Comer and Ross Dowd; *Property Men* A. Camp, Jimmy Cottrell, Jack DeGolconda, Bob Goodstein; *Makeup Supervisor* Wally Westmore; *Makeup Men* Harry Ray, Charlie Berner; *Prop Makers* Dick Parker, J. McFadden; *Hairdresser* Doris Harris; *Body Makeup Woman* Bonita White; *Wardrobe Men* J. Anderson and J. Balker; *Utility Laborer* Frank Grant and Bob Adams; *Transportation Cameraman* Loyal Griggs; *Painter* Wayne Buttress.

CAST

George Cochran	Bing Crosby
Harold Gridley	Bob Hope
Lalah	Dorothy Lamour
Ken Arok	Murvyn Vye

Gung	Peter Coe
Bhoma Da	Ralph Moody
Ramayana	Leon Askin
Specialty Dancer	Jack Claus
Bo Kassar	Bernie Gozier
Priest	Herman Cantor
Chief's Wife	Shela Fritz
Chief's Wife	Ethel K. Reiman
Chief's Wife	Irene K. Silva
Warriors	Charles Mauu
	Al Kikume
	Satini Puailoa
	Kuka L. Tuitama
Beautiful Girl in Basket	Mylee Haulani
Fat Woman in Basket	Kukhie Kuhns
Handmaidens	Pat Dane
	Sue Casey
	Patti McKaye
	Judith Landon
	Leslie Charles
	Jean Corbett
	Betty Onge
Guard	Michael Ansara
Lalah at Age Seven	Bunny Lewbel
Employment Agency Clerk	Donald Lawton
Attendant	Larry Chance
Verna's Father	Harry Cording
Eunice's Father	Roy Gordon
Conductor	Richard Keene
Eunice	Carolyn Jones
Verna	Jan Kayne
Eunice's Brother	Allan Nixon
Verna's Brother	Douglas Yorke
Wedding Attendant	Tony Urchel
Attendant	Fred Letuli
1st Youth Attendant	Johnny Leone
Old Crone	Mary Kanae
Boy	Raymond Lee
Boy	Luukia Luana
Lesser Priests	Bismark Auelua
	Bhogwan Singh
	Chanan Singh Sohi
	Jerry Groves
Themselves	Bob Crosby
	Dean Martin
	Jerry Lewis
	Jane Russell
	Humphrey Bogart

The Road to
Hong Kong, 1962

Dorothy Lamour had never been considered a third wheel during the first six films in the "Road" series, but with ten years having elapsed since *Road to Bali*, there were those who thought the vintage actress should be traded in for a sportier model.

The Road to Hong Kong caused a commotion. Not in terms of box-office attendance records (it was well received) or critical acclaim (most critics panned it), but rather in the controversy that surrounded Lamour and whether she would even be in the seventh "Road" picture.

Because nearly ten years had passed since the last "Road" film, many changes were made for what turned out to be the final picture in the series. Norman Panama and Melvin Frank were the producers, directors, writers, and part owners of the film; Paramount was replaced by United Artists; the movie was filmed in England; and although *Bali* had been filmed in color, *The Road to Hong Kong* was made in black and white. But, most notably, Dorothy Lamour lost her third spot in the billing.

Initially, gossip columnist Louella Parsons reported that Bob Hope and Bing Crosby would not use Dorothy Lamour as their love interest in the film. It was apparent Lamour was not being consulted from the beginning on the project, in that she began to read items in several columns that another "Road" film was going to be made in London. She read that because she had been in retirement for four or five years, Brigitte Bardot had first been considered for the role. In other reports, Gina Lollobrigida and Sophia Loren were the top choices to take up where the sarong-clad Lamour had left off.

As was the case in the last two films, Crosby and Hope each had a one-third share in the financing. This time they shared it with Frank and Panama, who wrote *Road to Utopia* in 1945 and were now producing and directing *Hong Kong* as well as having written the screenplay. It appeared that Crosby, Hope, Frank, and Panama had decided Lamour had been offscreen too long to be a major asset to the film. Lamour was, however, being offered a small part in the picture.

In her column, Parsons theorized that Lamour was considered too old for the role of the leading lady, despite the fact that she was younger than Hope or Crosby—almost ten years younger. The columnist believed that Lamour was a vital ingredient in the magical "Road" mixture, and she directly criticized Hope and Crosby for even considering dropping Lamour.

Meanwhile, preparations continued for the seventh "Road" picture, and eventually Norman Panama paid a visit to Lamour to let her read *The Road to Hong Kong* script and listen to a recording of "Warmer Than a Whisper," a song that Sammy Cahn had written for her.

Lamour said she understood how the powers-to-be might want a big box-office name to play opposite Crosby and Hope, but under no circumstances would she play a bit part in a "Road" picture. She had been a part of the frolicking threesome from the beginning and did not want her contribution to be regarded as insignificant.

Lamour listened to the song and then looked at the script. She could not find her part until she came to the script's end, where she had only a couple of pages of dialogue. Lamour was upset and told Panama she might consider the role if it were built up, but as it was, she was not interested.

A couple of weeks went by, and Melvin Frank called Lamour and indicated the movie was ready to go into production and that Crosby, Hope, Panama, and he would greatly appreciate it if she would join them in *The Road to Hong Kong*. Lamour repeated that she would participate only if he built up the part, but Frank claimed it was too late to make any further changes to the script. It was ironic that Frank, a veteran of the film series, should use such an excuse when the entire "Road" series had the reputation of scripts changing on an almost daily basis.

Hope also was upset that Lamour was not in the lead role and tempers reportedly erupted behind the scenes about the decision. Panama, Frank, and United Artists reasoned that Lamour was no longer the sexy, sarong-wearing lass of past films and that a younger actress would give the film more appeal. "Anyway," they argued, "Dorothy will still be in the movie making a guest appearance."

Dorothy Lamour (appearing as herself) in the musical number "Warmer Than a Whisper" with Bob Hope (playing Chester Babcock) in *The Road to Hong Kong* (1962).

That compromise satisfied Hope, but not Lamour. She turned the offer down after discovering the song they wanted her to sing would be "ruined" by a comedy sequence.

After more time had passed, Lamour finally found out why Panama and Frank had been so eager to have her be a part of the film. When the producers had made the distribution deal with United Artists, they had committed her name along with all the others. Even though they would sign someone else for the female lead, Lamour had to be included in the picture or the deal was off.

All during this time, Lamour kept hearing different stories: Crosby didn't want her in the film at all; Crosby did want her, but she didn't have a big enough following to play a major role; Hope had been fighting for her all along. It got to the point where she really did not know what to believe anymore.

In the end, the leading female role went to Britain's Joan Collins. (Collins would later gain fame on the *Dynasty* TV series.) And after Hope intervened, Lamour was persuaded to make a brief appearance as herself.

Lamour later was able to gloat a bit when the British press gave her a personal reception and sided with her regarding who should have been the leading lady. For *The Road to Hong Kong*, she did her little part, sang "Warmer Than a Whisper," and went home.

Almost as a premonition of things to come, Lamour had a line in *Hong Kong* that became all too real. In one scene, Hope and Crosby, donned in Oriental peasant garb, meet Lamour backstage in a theater where she is performing. Standing at her dressing-room door, they both start babbling excitedly about the predicament they are in. Lamour quiets them down and then asks: "Is that the plot of the picture so far?" Hope nods and says, "Right."

"I'd better hide you," she says.

"From the killers?" Hope asks.

"No," she responds, "from the critics."

In addition to all the upheaval regarding Lamour, the last "Road" was a complex film to make on other levels. To start with, it was being shot in three versions: one with American dialogue for the United States and Canada, another with anglicized lines for the United Kingdom, and a third without songs for the foreign language market. For instance, in one release, Crosby says, "Business first, fun and games later," while in another version, he says, "Business first, social activities later."

There also was the problem of placing Collins in the role that Lamour had occupied for many years. The sexy girl in the middle was a pivotal ingredient to any "Road" picture, and putting a new person in the role made it difficult to attain the same rapport as had been possible in the previous films. In *Hong Kong* the affinity never really came across onscreen, and an awkwardness almost always seemed to prevail.

The Road to Hong Kong was also troublesome to make because of the weather. Not that the London fog rolled in or it was generally inclement. Quite the contrary. The weather was too good most of the time. Too many warm, sunny days meant not enough Hope and Crosby. It seems that whenever four o'clock in the afternoon rolled around, the two would indicate that it was a beautiful day and off they would go.

Reportedly, Crosby sometimes worked without makeup on the exterior scenes of *Hong Kong* so that if there was any daylight left he could go hit a few golf shots. There were occasions when he even wore his golf attire underneath the clothes he was wearing in the picture, so all he had to do was rip off the outer wardrobe and take off to the course.

One day the two companions left the set in too much of a hurry. They had been shooting a harem scene during which Hope's toenails had been painted bright red. When Panama yelled "Cut!" at five o'clock, Hope scurried off with Crosby to the golf course for a fast nine holes, totally forgetting about the paint job on the toes of his feet.

Afterwards, as they sat down to change out of their golf shoes, two elderly English gentlemen sat across from them and began to eye Hope's bare feet. One of the gentlemen gave a shocked look and then nudged his partner to look at Hope's red toenails. Hope was unaware that his feet were being surveyed until one of the gentlemen inquired, "Mr. Crosby, is your friend in the ballet?" Hope put on his shoes and socks and ran out. It was probably the first time Crosby ever saw Hope embarrassed and stuck without a comeback.

For Crosby and Hope, the location was a great way for their families to spend some time together. The stars rented an old country home just outside London called Cranbourne Court, and Hope and his wife, Dolores, and his four children shared the place with Bing and Kathryn Crosby and their two youngsters.

In the morning, the singer and comedian would go off to work at the studio only about 15 minutes away while the wives and children explored England. At night they would all return to the mansion and have meals together. It was a harmonious existence for everyone and showed again how the Crosby-Hope relationship worked offscreen as well as on.

But the London location proved to be a hindrance when it came time to make a soundtrack recording of the film's songs several months later. On the original soundtrack recording, the word *love* at the end of the song "Let's Not Be Sensible" was not sung by Bing Crosby and had to be dubbed in later by somebody else.

This oversight came about because in the film there was some sort of visual distraction and Crosby never sang the last note of the song. The soundtrack recording of the song, however, could not be issued without the last note. By the time the situation was discovered, Crosby was long gone from the England studio, having hurried back to the United States to join his wife, Kathryn, and their new son, Nathaniel. Rather than try to arrange to get him back, the recording studio simply hired someone else to sing the note. Mike Sammes, of the Mike Sammes Singers group, was working on an album and was called in to supply the missing word.

Crosby's voice being dubbed on one word was not the only thing that changed regarding the songs in the last "Road" film. For *The Road to Hong Kong* the songwriting team was different as a result of the death of lyricist Johnny Burke in the mid–1950s. Burke had been with Crosby since *Pennies from Heaven* (1936) and, in addition to the "Road" tunes, had written the lyrics to such songs as "I've Got a Pocketful of Dreams" and "An Apple for the Teacher." The Burke/Van Heusen partnership lasted 15 years, 14 Crosby pictures (five of them "Road" films), and nearly 50 hit songs.

Despite Burke's death, the show went on, and the lively lyricist Sammy Cahn replaced Burke in the Jimmy Van Heusen partnership.

For *The Road to Hong Kong*, Cahn and Van Heusen wrote Lamour's "Warmer Than a Whisper" and "Teamwork," which became another Hope/Crosby team classic. The song scribes also wrote the title tune and Crosby's "Let's Not Be Sensible," which he performed with Collins. But the songs paled in comparison to the earlier Burke and Van Heusen hits.

Also not up to par was the directing. Norman Panama and his partner Melvin Frank had the longest association with the "Road" pictures and their personnel, first as radio writers for Hope, then as screenwriters for two "Road" pictures (*Utopia* and *Hong Kong*), and then as producers of *Hong Kong*, which Panama directed.

Panama began his writing career in Hollywood in 1938 when he and Frank worked as radio writers for Groucho Marx and Rudy Vallee. Most of his success came while teamed with Frank in one capacity or another. Panama was coproducer and coscreenwriter (with Frank) for Cary Grant's *Mr. Blandings Builds His Dream House* (1948). Panama also cowrote (with Frank and Norman Krasna) Crosby's *White Christmas* (1954), costarring Danny Kaye.

But for *The Road to Hong Kong*, the leads were aging and the physical comedy which had been so prevalent in the early films no longer worked effectively. Panama, as the director, could do nothing to recapture the magic of the previous six films. As instrumental as Panama and Frank might have been in other capacities, as a director, Panama added little to the series.

Panama and Frank did, however, create a line in the film that no one thought would get past the censors. In *Hong Kong*, Peter Sellers did a one-day cameo as a doctor from India who tries to cure Hope's loss of memory. In the scene, Hope is sitting on an examining table in the doctor's office and Sellers, in a black Nehru jacket and stethoscope, asks Hope to read an eye chart. When Hope can't read the chart because it is printed in a foreign language, Sellers says, "I'll play it for you."

Sellers picks up a reed instrument and adroitly plays the eye chart as if it were sheet music. A snake slowly emerges from a nearby woven basket, and Sellers charms it with melodic tones from the instrument. Hope asks the doctor what he would have done if the snake had bit him.

"Very simple," says Sellers in a stilted East Indian dialect. "I simply cut the wound and suck out the poison."

"But what if it's in a place you can't reach with your mouth?" Hope asks.

"That," Sellers says, "is when you find out who your friends are."

Hope later talked to Panama and Frank about including the line in the film. "You can't do that joke," he said to the writers. "It's based on a very well-known dirty story."

Panama and Frank insisted on leaving the joke in the picture, and at a preview showing of *The Road to Hong Kong* the joke got a full 30-second laugh. Either the censors were laughing along with everyone else or they didn't know the well-known dirty story.

As for the film itself, it was a bit of an embarrassment. The flimsy plot features Chester Babcock (Hope) and Harry Turner (Crosby) as vaudevillians wanted for fraud, this time in Hong Kong. Like *Utopia*, which Panama and Frank also wrote, *Hong Kong* is told in flashback. The movie opens with Hope and Crosby in a space capsule as Joan Collins is relating to government officials the recent events leading to their present situation.

The main story twist is that Hope has mentally absorbed all the numbers of a rocket-fuel formula but has suffered amnesia. Much of the movie is spent with Hope and Crosby trying to find cures that will bring his memory back. A gang of ruthless power-seekers called the Third Echelon, led by Robert Morley, try to obtain the secret formula before the United States or Russia. Collins at first is part of the villainous conspiracy, but then she becomes fond of the boys, realizes Morley is a madman, and defects to help Hope and Crosby.

The standard series of wild ventures results in launches into outer space and chases into the underworld. Toward the end of the film, Hope and Crosby blunder into a vaudeville act which stars Dorothy Lamour as herself. They use her costumes, appear on stage during her number, and eventually use her car as a getaway vehicle.

At the very end of the film, Crosby, Collins, and Hope, in their effort to escape the villains, wind up traveling in a spaceship to another planet. There they go into a reprise of the song "Teamwork," with which Crosby and Hope opened the film. As Hope sings, Crosby and Collins end in a clinch and Hope tries to break it up by calling for special effects. Instead, Hope is hauled into the air via special effects and ends up hanging there as the picture ends.

Although the film was moderately received by audiences, most critics thought it was one "Road" too many. The *New York Times* critic wrote: "All in all, you felt they enjoyed getting together again, and you wish them well. The effect on the screen is rather embarrassing, however." Archer Winston of the *New York Post* softened the truth and noted kindly: "Give them an 'A' for effort; then suit yourself about attending." *Variety* was a little more kind: "Perhaps the old formula creaks occasionally, but not enough to cause any disappointment while the zany situations and razor-edge wisecracks keep the whole affair bubbling happily."

Like *Road to Bali, The Road to Hong Kong* had quite an array of guest stars. But unlike its predecessor, *Hong Kong* also displayed some talented and distinguished supporting players. Aside from newcomer Joan Collins, who would go on to TV fame in *Dynasty* and who appeared in such films as *Stopover Tokyo* (1957), *Rally 'Round the Flag, Boys!* (1958), and *Warning Shot* (1966), *The Road to Hong Kong* featured the distinguished British actor Robert Morley. Morley was nominated for a Best Supporting Actor Academy Award for his role in *Marie Antoinette* (1938). He also appeared in *Major Barbara* (1941), *The African Queen* (1951), and *Topkapi* (1964).

Another English star in *Hong Kong* was Peter Sellers, who was nominated for a Best Actor Academy Award for *Dr. Strangelove, or How I Learned to Stop Worrying and Love the Bomb* (1964).

Sellers is probably best known for his role of Inspector Jacques Clouseau in the series of Pink Panther films of the 1960s and 1970s, including *The Pink Panther* (1964), *A Shot in the Dark* (1964), and *The Pink Panther Strikes Again* (1976). He also appeared in *Lolita* (1962), *What's New, Pussycat?* (1965), and *Murder by Death* (1976).

Other cast members in *The Road to Hong Kong* include Walter Gotell, Roger Delgado, Felix Aylmer, and Peter Madden. Cameos included Jerry Colonna (in his last film), David Niven, Zsa Zsa Gabor, Dean Martin, and Frank Sinatra.

And, as with all the "Road" films, the laughs were not all on the screen. There was one scene in which Zsa Zsa Gabor played a nurse who was trying to cure Hope of amnesia. She was to say, "I think I can get him to talk," then give Hope a big kiss. Panama, who was directing, ordered the scene to begin. Gabor gave Hope the kiss, then silence.

"Cut!" Panama said. "Bob—you were supposed to say a line there."

"I can't talk with one lip," Hope gulped, breaking up the crew and the other actors.

It was the cameo appearances that were in some cases the highlights of the film. At the film's end, Hope, Crosby, and Collins, still in their Oriental peasant attire, are on another planet. As usual, the two leads are arguing over who will get the leading lady, and they finally devise a plan.

"Mondays, Wednesdays, and Fridays you come to my house," says Crosby.

"Yeah, Tuesdays, Thursdays, and Saturdays, my house," says Hope.

"What about Sundays?" asks Collins, to which Hope replies: "Everybody rests."

Meanwhile, two astronauts, in the form of Frank Sinatra and Dean Martin in jumpsuits and old-fashioned aviator hats, come along. Immediately Collins is off hugging and kissing them. Hope and Crosby eliminate the two intruders by calling for "Special Effects" and Sinatra and Martin are lifted up into the air and out of the scene.

Special effects were evident in *Hong Kong* as much as any of the other "Road" films, but in this case the script had the leads calling attention to their use. In addition to the final scene with the astronauts, Hope, Crosby, and Collins make a costume change in the middle of the film simply by calling for special effects. In the scene in a Hong Kong street, Hope is wearing a smoking jacket and dark slacks, Crosby a white shirt and dark slacks, and Collins a long white gown. In a split second, they are immediately adorned in peasant Hong Kong attire.

Although there are some genuinely funny bits in *Hong Kong*, (as when Hope and Crosby are decked out in spacesuits made for monkeys and must eat from a banana- and milk-feeding machine that goes haywire on the spaceship), the amount of slapstick comedy was reduced for the most part. It was, admitted Hope at the time, just a matter of age.

"I find that with the increasing years you can't do the hokum," said Hope. "It looks a little silly to do some of the things that you would do. And Bing and I are conscious of that. Although we're doing our same characters, we're not doing as many physical things. I think the public expects this type of performance because they know you; you're

Chester Babcock (Bob Hope) takes Diane (Joan Collins) and Harry Turner (Bing Crosby) for a ride in the 1962 film *The Road to Hong Kong*.

on television; you're in their eye all the time ... they know your age practically and they don't want you acting too silly."

Hope was 58 and Crosby 60. *Hong Kong* would be the last "Road" the pair would travel together. Most critics felt it was simply "one 'Road' too many."

Still, the film was a box-office smash, as some of the "Road" magic remained with the rapport and timing between the two stars still evident. Early in the film, the native pilot of a makeshift flying machine called "Fly It Yourself" quits his job, and Crosby tries to con Hope into flying the apparatus. Crosby starts his influential patter as he helps Hope put on a silver flying jacket and silver helmet with a tiny propeller on top. Hope, of course, wants no part of it.

"I got a flash for you about Fly It Yourself," says Hope.

"What?" queries Crosby.

"Fly it yourself."

The self-deprecating humor and references not related to the plot that surfaced in other "Road" films also remained in *Hong Kong*. In one scene, Hope and Crosby eye a shark while in the underwater headquarters of the Third Echelon.

"Don't worry," says Crosby, "they don't eat people."

"What about actors?" asks Hope.

"We're safe," says Crosby.

Even the patty-cake routine worked this time around as Hope and Crosby elude officials of a remote religious order by using the technique.

But as for the plot and performances, *Hong Kong* was the poorest "Road" picture of the lot. Part of what was lacking in *The Road to Hong Kong* was believability. In all the other films, it was at least conceivable that these footloose adventurers could end up in exotic and unchartered lands, and that aspect added to the allure of the films. In *The Road to Hong Kong*, the trip in the space capsule suspended all belief in reality and made the whole film harder to like and accept. And for that reason, it does not hold up as well as the others.

Hope and Crosby also just seemed to be going through the motions in the film. Twenty-two years had somehow slipped by, and the sharp-witted wanderers simply could not maintain the high standard of the earlier films.

The Road to Hong Kong
Melnor Films Ltd.
Released by United Artists

Released: May 1962
Running time: 91 minutes

Producer Melvin Frank; *Production Supervisor* William Kirby; *Production Secretary* Inez Easton; *Production Designer* Roger Furse; *Director* Norman Panama; *1st Assistant Director* Bluey Hill; *2d Assistant Directors* Gordon Gilbert, Edward Dorian, Ken Softley; *Written by* Norman Panama and Melvin Frank; *Animation* Biographic Cartoon Films; *Director of Photography* Jack Hilyard; *Art Directors* Sydney Cain, Bill Hutchinson; *Assistant Art Director* Bob Cartwright; *Special Effects* Wally Veevers, Ted Samuels; *Editorial Supervisor* Alan Osbiston; *Camera Operator* Gerry Fisher; *Camera Grip* Frank Howard; *Film Editor* John Victor Smith; *1st Assistant Editor* Joan Morduch; *2d Assistant Editor* Ray Thorne; *Songs by* Sammy Cahn and Jimmy Van Heusen; *Musical Numbers Staged by* Jack Baker and Sheila Meyers; *Music Composer and Conductor* Robert Farnon; *Musical Associates* Bill McGuffie, Doug Gamley; *Sound* A.G. Ambler, Bob Jones,

Red Law; *Sound Editor* Chris Greenham; *Music Editor* Lee Doig; *Costume Designer* Anthony Mendleson; *Continuity* Angela Martelli, Pamela Davies; *Makeup* Dave Aylott, Eric Allwright; *Hairdressing* Joan White, Joyce James; *Wardrobe Mistress* May Walding; *Wardrobe Master* Ernie Farrer; *Main Title Designer* Maurice Binder; *Set Decoration* Maurice Fowler; *Scenic Artist* Basil Mannin; *Boom Operator* Peter Dukelow; *Sound Camera Operator* Jimmy Dooley.

CAST

Harry Turner	Bing Crosby
Chester Babcock	Bob Hope
Diane	Joan Collins
Dorothy Lamour	Herself
The Leader	Robert Morley
Dr. Zorbb	Walter Gotell
Jhinnah	Roger Delgado
Grand Lama	Felix Aylmer
Lama	Peter Madden
American Officials	Alan Gifford
	Robert Ayres
	Robin Hughes
Doctor	Julian Sherrier
Agent	Bill Nagy
Photographer	Guy Standeven
Messenger	John McCarthy
Servant	Simon Levy
Chinese Girl	Mei Ling
Receptionist	Katya Douglas
Nubians	Harry Baird
	Irving Allen
Lady at Airport	Jacqueline Jones
Leader's Men	Victor Brooks
	Roy Patrick
	John Dearth
	David Randall
	Michael Wynn
Girls	Yvonne Shima
	Camilla Brockman
	Lena Margot
	Sheree Winton
	Edwina Carroll
	Diane Valentine
	April Ashley
	Jacqueline Leigh
	Sein Short
	Lier Hwang

CAST

	Michele Mok
	Zoe Zephyr
Guest Stars	Peter Sellers
	Frank Sinatra
	Dean Martin
	David Niven
	Zsa Zsa Gabor
	Jerry Colonna

The Final Road

The Crosby/Hope/Lamour series consisted of seven films, but there were a myriad of "Roads" that never came to be, for one reason or another.

According to Lamour, in the mid–1940s Paramount announced that because it was becoming too difficult to arrange Crosby's, Hope's, and her schedules, the still unreleased *Road to Utopia* would be the last of the "Road" pictures. As a result of the announcement, Paramount was flooded with more than 75,000 letters of protest. Another announcement was quickly made that the studio was considering another "Road" film after all. This one would cast Hope and Crosby as a couple of GI Joes returning to the girl they left behind. It had the tentative title "Road to Home," but nothing ever came of it.

According to some accounts, two additional "Road" films were proposed after *The Road to Hong Kong*. One was "Road to the Moon," which was, reportedly, to costar Marilyn Monroe, and the other was titled "Road to Bombay." These plans also never materialized.

There also was a "Road to Moscow," which was more in the imagination of writers Frank Butler and Don Hartman than anywhere else. (See pages 41–42.)

Unlike some other film comedy teams such as Martin and Lewis and Abbott and Costello, Bob Hope and Bing Crosby never really dissolved their film partnership and "broke up the act." In fact, plans were in the works for an eighth "Road" picture at the time of Crosby's death in 1977.

A story had been created and a script was written called "Road to Tomorrow," but the title was later changed to "Road to the Fountain of Youth." Mel Shavelson, who was slated to direct the film, would finally be getting his name on the "Road" credits, after years of supplying unbilled jokes for the series while part of Hope's writing team. Hope, Crosby, and Lamour had all agreed to appear in the film, and shooting locations were planned in England, Saudi Arabia, and Moscow.

Understandably, Lamour was a tad cautious about the new film because she had been virtually ignored during preparations for *Hong Kong*. She was making a good living again as a stage actress, however, and this time she was being consulted from the start on the project.

"Road … to the Fountain of Youth" was to be a spoof of all past "Road" pictures and, like all the others, the plot was simple. It was to start out with Crosby and Hope meeting each other again while taking their grandchildren to the airport. They would spend some time lying to each other about how good they looked at their age, and before you knew it, they would be on a plane to London and off on another mystery. Of course, along the way they would bump into Lamour.

So 1977 should have been a good year for the "Road" team. Crosby had already arranged a tour of Europe, kicked off at the London Palladium, and, besides the planned film, a London-based record company wanted Hope and Crosby to make a duet album. In addition, Hope agreed to help Crosby celebrate 50 years in show business at a gala tribute televised at Pasadena's Ambassador Auditorium in March.

But the televised concert in Pasadena on March 3 changed all the plans for that year. Twelve hundred friends of Crosby's were seated in the audience watching him sing his final song alone on stage, giving him a standing ovation at its conclusion.

As Crosby started to leave the stage, he lost his footing and sagged into a prop wall which masked an orchestra pit. Crosby's weight was too much for the flimsy wall, and he crashed through it. Crosby plunged 25 feet into a concrete-floored orchestra pit, severely crushing a disc in his spine, making him a virtual invalid for months.

Plans for starting work on the new film were altered when it became obvious that Crosby's injuries were more serious than first thought. He was well enough, however, to undertake his previously arranged autumn tour of Britain and a two-week run at the Palladium. But because his recovery was so much slower than expected, the picture had to be postponed indefinitely.

Bing Crosby died on October 14, 1977, when he suffered a fatal heart attack on a golf course in Spain. Crosby's death brought to an end one of the most charming and enduring film series in motion picture history.

Stopping by the Side of the Road: An Overview of the "Road" Series

Series comedies have been around for a long time. Like any successful business, Hollywood has often tried to find a basic product that it could sell time and time again. So sequels and even series of films featuring the same stars have always been a desirable, as well as a profitable, path for motion picture studio executives to follow.

Film series often come to fruition from very different angles. Some are established from other media, such as comic strip characters. This was the case in the Blondie film series that lasted 12 years (1938–50) and consisted of 28 movies. The series starred Penny Singleton as Blondie and Arthur Lake as Dagwood Bumstead.

Only after the first picture is successful does a series become an option. This was the case with the "Road" films and also the Andy Hardy films starring Mickey Rooney. There were a total of 16 movies in the very popular series, which began in 1937 with *A Family Affair* and ended in 1958 with *Andy Hardy Comes Home*. Over the years, other avenues of show business have been mined for possible film display. The advent of Burns and Allen in films came about as a direct result of their appearances on radio. Dean Martin and Jerry Lewis came to the movies via their nightclub act, and the Marx Brothers appeared on screen as a result of their Broadway shows. In fact, the Marx Brothers' first two films, *The Cocoanuts* (1929, Paramount) and *Animal Crackers* (1930, Paramount), were successful stage plays starring the brothers before they were made into movies.

Still other series are designed for specific audiences. The youth-oriented Henry Aldrich series (1939–44) ran through 11 movies. The

Beach Party films in the early 1960s, starring Frankie Avalon and Annette Funicello, also were pitched directly to the youth audience.

The most successful series were built around the chemistry between the actors, such as the Marx Brothers, Martin and Lewis, and Abbott and Costello. It is no wonder, then, that the "Road" movies were so popular. Unlike most other series, the "Roads" spread over a 22-year period, while most others tended to come out of the studios on an assembly-line basis. Abbott and Costello, for example, made 36 movies over a 16-year period, averaging more than two movies per year. The "Road" films as a series were a cut above the rest. The films were of a slightly higher quality, featured bigger name stars, and, as the series progressed, were produced in a more careful fashion.

Although Dorothy Lamour played an integral part in the team throughout the series, it was the lively banter of Hope and Crosby that audiences remember the most. In many ways, the Crosby/Hope combination in the "Road" pictures made them the premiere film comedy team of their day; they hold their own against other popular film teams of the time such as Abbott and Costello, the Marx Brothers, and later, Martin and Lewis.

In terms of specialties, Crosby and Hope were similar to Dean Martin and Jerry Lewis, who made 16 films together between 1949 and 1956. Both teams had exceptional singers and hilarious comedians as partners. But that, for the most part, is where the similarity ends.

For the humor aspect, Martin was the straight man, often the bully, and Lewis was the pitied character, the schnook. That was not the case in the "Road" films. Although Hope was often the sympathetic, put-upon character, it was often at least partly his own doing. A stateroom scene on an ocean liner in *Road to Utopia* is evidence of Hope's characters bringing about some of their own misfortune. After he and Crosby debate who will hang on to the bankroll of money they have accumulated, Hope firmly declares that they will just put the money in the safe. He opens a tiny porthole in the stateroom, which he assumes is a safe, and tosses the money out into the ocean waves.

Portions of the two acts also were similar. Early in their careers, Martin and Lewis would offer unsolicited comments to the other entertainer during a performance. They played straight for each other, intentionally stepped on each other's lines, and raised general bedlam.

Hope and Crosby often commented about each other's performances, but it was more spontaneous. They also often set each other up for the jokes. In some ways they were two straight men and two comedians who alternated roles. With the constant ad-libbing done by the pair, the straight line for a joke was sometimes produced unwittingly. In a regular comedy team, almost everything is planned out and rehearsed. If there are ad-libs, most are within the framework of the sketch or routine. Not so with Hope and Crosby.

In their films, the Crosby-Hope duo also alternated as romantic leads. Although the sentimental strains of Crosby's voice secured his position as the premiere romantic in the "Road" films, Hope was always a close second. Although it was a running gag that Crosby always got Lamour or the leading lady in the "Road" pictures, it was not all that one-sided. Hope wound up with the leading lady several times in the final reel, even if it was by chance or chicanery.

In *Road to Singapore*, Crosby gets Lamour after Hope and Lamour have gone off together. Hope realizes that he and Lamour are only friends and she really loves Crosby. "You're the dopey-looking cluck she wants," says Hope to Crosby in the film.

Crosby successfully woos Lamour in *Road to Zanzibar*, but Hope earns the favor of Una Merkel as the four are trying to earn their passage back to America by doing a vaudeville-style magic act. The same holds true in *Road to Morocco*, in which Crosby walks away with Lamour, but Hope again gets a consolation prize, this time in the form of Dona Drake.

In *Road to Utopia*, a glacier separates Hope and Crosby, and Hope marries Lamour, only to adopt a son who looks astonishingly like Crosby. Hope gets the girl again in *Road to Rio*, after using a swinging pendant to hypnotize Lamour into marrying him. But Crosby gains his revenge in *Road to Bali*, winding up with two girls—Lamour and Jane Russell—as Hope tries to avert the end of the picture.

In *The Road to Hong Kong*, it appears at first that Hope and Crosby will have to share leading lady Joan Collins. In the final scene, however, Crosby and Collins are in a clinch while Hope is suspended high in the air above them, courtesy of "special effects."

Having Lamour as the same female lead throughout most of the pictures also helped the comedy duo. Martin and Lewis worked with a different leading lady in nearly every film, from Donna Reed to Shirley MacLaine, but after making several films with Lamour in the pivotal third person spot, Crosby and Hope knew exactly what to expect of her as a performer. This helped greatly with their timing and delivery. In addition, Lamour had a somewhat stabilizing effect on the team, making them more readily believable characters. As funny as Crosby and Hope were, they were never quite as zany as the Marx Brothers on screen.

As indicated in *The Road to Hong Kong* chapter, part of the difficulty in making that film was working leading lady Joan Collins into the third person spot formerly held by Lamour. If the boys had had to do that in every picture with a different female lead each time, the results would not have been as smooth and flawless.

Aside from having a variety of female leads in their movies, Martin and Lewis also differed from Crosby and Hope in the characters they portrayed in the films. In all instances in the "Road" films, Hope and Crosby are friendly competitors, vying for the same gorgeous girl or trying to abscond with the other's money. Martin and Lewis characters were nothing like that in their films. In most cases, Lewis was the schnook who looked after Martin, who was usually cast as an ungrateful or conceited individual. And, especially as the Martin and Lewis films progressed, more and more scenes were shot without the other in them. That was rarely the case with Hope and Crosby. Except for their time on film when one or the other is wooing some luscious female, Hope and Crosby appear together in the films a great deal of the time.

In terms of the characters they portrayed on film, Crosby and Hope were most like Abbott and Costello. Much of the Abbott and Costello comedy was derived from the idea of the common man caught in peculiar circumstances. Whether it be battling a bullying sergeant in their first hit *Buck Privates* (1941) or warding off menacing monsters in *Abbott and Costello Meet Frankenstein* (1948), the majority of their comedy was delivered from their reactions to their unusual situations.

Similarly, though not to as great a comedic crescendo, Hope and Crosby were average guys caught in exotic and foreign locales. They, like Abbott and Costello, clowned their way out of the conflicts, though much more subtly and effectively. Harry Tugend, who produced *Road to Bali*, once explained the basic formula for the "Road" pictures this way: "Get 'em up a tree; throw rocks at 'em; then get 'em out of the tree."

Abbott and Costello were very much a "comedy team"—a straight man and a comic—whereas Crosby and Hope were two entertainers who worked together doing comedy, as well as music.

Music was the other main difference in the "Road" team films versus the Abbott and Costello flicks. As a comedy team, the skinny-fat duo did not perform musical numbers. If there was any music in their films, it was provided by guest stars like the Andrews Sisters or

Dick Foran. On the other hand, Hope and Crosby, with Lamour, were a complete musical comedic package.

Although popular with audiences, Abbott and Costello were never received very well by the critics because they used dated material. They relied on humor from vaudeville and burlesque, and they did not vary it to accommodate changes in society. Although Crosby and Hope were known to trot out old routines from vaudeville days, at least the Hope/Crosby references outside the plot were always topical. That kept their humor fresh and alive.

While filming the "Road" pictures, Hope, Crosby, and Lamour had their zany moments, but most of them were probably off camera rather than on. Not so for the Marx Brothers. Their comedic escapades were wild and riotous in the 13 films they made together from 1929 to 1949.

The team of the three Marx Brothers excelled in various areas of comedy. Groucho was superb with puns and nonsense patter, while Groucho and Chico had conversations that revealed logic could somehow be found in illogical thinking. Harpo was a master of sight gags. Because the trio started on Broadway, they played things more expansively in order to get them across on stage. By contrast, Hope and Crosby, both radio veterans, were more subdued, more attuned to setting up a joke or sight gag and then hitting the punch line.

In some ways the Marx Brothers films were predecessors to some of the "Road" picture comedy. As famous as the asides to the audience were in the "Road" films, the idea did not originate in that series.

The Marx Brothers, particularly Groucho, also did asides to the audience. In a scene from *Horse Feathers* (1932, Paramount), Chico is about to play the piano when Groucho looks at the camera and says, "I have to stay here, but there's no reason why you folks can't go out to the lobby until this thing blows over." The quip was astonishingly similar to Hope's reference to Crosby, who was about to sing in *Road to Bali* some 20 years later.But whereas Groucho always had some snide remark, Hope and Crosby often presented their comments as if the audience was in on the joke.

The music in the Marx Brothers films bore some resemblance to that of the "Road" pictures. As talented musicians, Chico on the piano and Harpo on the harp could play beautifully. Their musical talent was on the same distinguished level as Crosby's singing. As for humorous songs, Groucho handled them as effectively as any of the patter duets or trios in the "Road" films.

But in terms of romantic ballads, the Marx Brothers could not compete with Crosby and Lamour. As was the case with Abbott and Costello, when something needed to be sung in a serious vein, the Marx Brothers brought in someone like Alan Jones to warble the tunes.

As is often the case in Hollywood, successful films spawn imitations. One Paramount film with Dorothy Lamour was even considered by some to be a spinoff of the "Road" series.

In *Rainbow Island* (1944, Paramount), Lamour plays a white girl brought up on the Pacific island by her doctor father. Merchant marines Barry Sullivan, Eddie Bracken, and Gil Lamb land on the island while escaping from the Japanese. Only because Bracken resembles a native god are the white men spared from sacrificial death. The aspects of Lamour as a native, the forced comedy, and the exotic locales made the resemblance to the "Road" films undeniable.

On other studio lots, like Warner Brothers, the "jumping on the bandwagon" was even more obvious. Warner Brothers screen veterans Dennis Morgan and Jack Carson were teamed in the short "Two Guys" series. The first film, *Two Guys from Milwaukee* (1946, Warner Bros.), centers on a young Balkan prince who goes incognito in Brooklyn and befriends a cab driver. The rambunctious comedy had an amiable cast which included Joan Leslie, Janis Paige, and several gag guest appearances.

The second and final flick in the series was *Two Guys from Texas* (1948, Warner Bros.). In this film two vaudevillians (Morgan and Carson) find themselves on the run from crooks. The plot was not much more than a peg on which to hang some clowning and a few musical numbers. Also in the cast were Dorothy Malone and Penny Edwards.

Both "Two Guys" films were directed by "Road" veteran David Butler, but there was no way these films could compete with the likes of a Crosby/Hope "Road" feature.

The reasons for the success of the "Road" series are as varied as the exotic locales to which the trio traveled. While some variables such as scripts, songs, and comedic timing are readily apparent, others, like the best way to film a comedy scene, may not be as easily observed.

Most comedic filmmakers agree that often in comedy, the best way to film the action is to keep things as simple as possible. Comedy usually works best if seen straight, with a person delivering a straight line and a comic reacting to it. In film parlance, this is commonly called a two-shot, where the subject of the shot is two people.

Two examples of this simplicity in the "Road" pictures, with a minor alteration, are the lip-sync scene in *Road to Morocco* and the patty-cake routine throughout the entire film series.

In *Road to Morocco*, dehydrated Hope and Crosby are in the desert when they meet up with a mirage of Dorothy Lamour. The three start singing "Moonlight Becomes You," and the camera stays on the three stars (a three-shot) with occasional close-ups of one star or the another. The comedic element of the scene is that each star is singing with another's voice. Lamour sings with Crosby's voice, Hope with Lamour's, and Crosby with Hope's. The scene is set in the desert, with nothing around except sky and sand. The words of the song coming out of unexpected mouths, and the facial expressions of the three stars are the comedy. There are no extraneous scenery, movements, or sets to distract from it.

The famous patty-cake routines throughout the films are yet another example of film comedy photography. When Hope and Crosby set themselves up to unload on the bad guy, it is usually a simple three-shot of the heavy in the center and the stars on either side. They go through the patty-cake routine and flatten, or are flattened by, their adversary. Only then does the scene expand to include the ensuing fracas that breaks out. If the patty-cake bit was shown as a small portion of a larger scene rather than by itself, it would lose much of its effectiveness.

Although simplicity may be essential in filming comedic bits, it was not the key when it came to costumes in the "Road" pictures. The costumes used in the "Road" series were an important part of the series' success.

In motion pictures, costumes are not just frills added to enhance an illusion. Very often the style of a costume can suggest a certain psychological state. In the "Road" series, the jaunty sailor caps, casual shirts, and baggy pants worn by Bing Crosby and Bob Hope in several films reflected the lackadaisical airs of the roles they played in these films. Similarly, when the team is in the midst of foreign royalty in *Road to Morocco* or *Road to Bali* they are adorned in wondrous turbans, silks, and flowing robes, all of which added to the sense of the enchantment of the land.

Early on in the series, mainly because of budget constraints, costumes were more modest. In *Road to Singapore*, Hope and Crosby wore khaki pants, sailing caps, and pullover or button-down shirts through most of the movie. Lamour may not have always been in a sarong, but she spent most of the film in the same simple blouse and skirt. Even in an island banquet scene midway through the film, the Hope and Crosby characters use drapes from their hut to wrap themselves up like natives. The costume is so simple that it could, indeed, have been left-over drapery material.

But once the films started to become successful and the budgets expanded, they went all out with costuming. Not only did Lamour's gowns become more glamorous, but the two male leads also dressed up in more exotic garb.

The dressing up was fine with Hope, but Crosby often did not like it, according to Edith Head, the Oscar-winning costume designer.

"He didn't mind anything that was masculine," said Head, "for instance a Scottish kilt, but if you tried to get him into something that was a little costumey, he'd say 'Don't these look a little ornate?' In *Road to Morocco* he wasn't terribly fond of the turbans and silks."

The costumes added to the exotic locales of the films, whether it be the deserts of Morocco or the shores of Bali, and added greatly to the allure and appeal of the films. During the war-filled days of the early 1940s, anything that helped audiences think of faraway places and distant locales was welcome. The costuming in the "Road" films aided in that escape. Costumes convey ideas and emotions, and in the "Road" films the ideas were communicated effectively by what the actors wore.

Movie sets also communicate certain feelings or ideas, often as an extension of a theme. The climactic scene in *Road to Utopia* points out how setting can play an important part in the plot. As Hope and Crosby are chased out onto the frozen wasteland, a crack in the ice pack develops and separates Lamour and Hope on one side and Crosby and the villains on the other. Hope and Lamour go off together, and Crosby is left to battle the bad guys. The physical distance of the gaping chasm visually instills in viewers the idea that there is no way they will bridge the gap. Their lives are forced to take separate paths.

The sets of the "Road" pictures also were another way in which filmmakers could transport audiences to foreign lands. The sets could appear however directors saw them because few in the audience really knew what Bali or Singapore looked like. As long as the art directors and designers were able to come up with a reasonable facsimile of the imagined exotic locale, everyone was content. Most moviegoers knew only what they saw on the screen.

An example of shooting a scene for believability is evidenced in *Road to Utopia*. In the film, Hope and Crosby are scaling mountain sides in the Alaskan territory. The mountains in reality were no far-ther than the nearest studio soundstage. The street scenes in *Utopia* were probably an unused cowboy set on the back lot of Paramount. Still, in the magic of the movies, it all becomes real and totally believable.

Also believable in the "Road" films were the stunts and fight scenes. As indicated in previous chapters, the scenes in the "Road" films often became a bit hazardous for the stars. Two examples are the horses charging down the street in *Road to Morocco* and the crooner and comedian falling backwards while hanging on a rope in *Road to Utopia*. With big stars who were often Number 1 and Number 2 at the box office in any given year, stunt doubles were often used in the "Road" pictures.

This use of stunt doubles was especially interesting early on when budgets may not have been as sizable as in later films. In some fight scenes in *Road to Singapore*, for example, the actors standing in for Crosby and Hope struggle to keep their caps on because if their head-gear fell off, it would be readily apparent that these two were not Hope and Crosby, but stunt doubles. If the caps had flown off, the scene would have had to be reshot, and that would have cost the studio money. Fortunately, in this and other scenes throughout the series, the stuntmen were able to pull it off and keep the scenes believable.

The songs in the "Road" films also helped the pictures succeed. Today, some 50 years after many of the songs were introduced, "Moon-light Becomes You" or "But Beautiful" can still be heard on radio sta-tions or compact discs across America.

The consistency of good songs throughout the series was possi-ble, in part, because only five composers or lyricists worked on the seven "Road" pictures. The other factor that enabled the high quality of songs to be maintained was that these were genuinely talented indi-viduals.

Among the musical marvels lending their melodious abilities to the series were lyricist Sammy Cahn (*The Road to Hong Kong*) and composer James V. Monaco (*Road to Singapore*). Even director Victor Schertzinger wrote the music for two songs in the first "Road" picture. James Van Heusen was the most frequently used composer, contribut-ing music for six films. But the one man who was there at the begin-ning and through almost the entire series was lyricist Johnny Burke. His presence helped maintain high quality and consistency in the musi-cal scores of the "Road" pictures.

As good as these songs were, it was the aptitude of the stars which helped the tunes gain acceptance and attain hit status. When Van Heusen worked on the set of the *Road to Zanzibar*, he saw how Hope and Crosby clowned and how deftly their banter was captured in the finished film. He spent considerable time with Crosby as the film was put together, listening to him negotiate the pretty phrases of "It's Always You," and he watched cheerfully as Crosby hammered home the verbal and musical humor of "You Lucky People, You."

Hope deserves credit for holding his own since the hoofer-turned-comedian always ranked third in the music area. Crosby and Lamour were the singers, and they had song-writing help and musical arrangers on all sides in the "Road" series. Hope was able to deliver a song with style and personality, carry a tune and harmonize very well ... a perfect complement to the other two vocalists.

Like the films themselves, the "Road" songs endure. That, for the most part, can be attributed to the talented songwriters and musical professionals who worked on the "Road" films. Hope and Crosby excelled as a team by combining song, dance, ad-libbed humor, and detailed characterizations into artistically meaningful and wildly popular motion pictures. The songs lingered on, even though the series came to an end.

The Crooner Goes to Hollywood: The Movies of Bing Crosby

The laid-back style of Bing Crosby as a singer carried over nicely into film. But the easygoing sojourning character he portrayed in the "Road" films did not emerge without a few false starts.

Crosby came to movies by way of an orchestra, the Paul Whiteman Orchestra, to be exact. In the late 1920s, Crosby was part of a trio known as the Rhythm Boys (Al Rinker and Harry Barris were the others). With Whiteman, Crosby gained valuable show business experience and exposure in vaudeville and on the big-band circuit.

The three Rhythm Boys were all in their mid–twenties, and being rather young, they tended to be somewhat irresponsible. Sometimes they did not show up for appearances, and often they did not prepare any new performance material. Unfortunately, the type of singing act that they were doing depended upon creating new material all the time. Needless to say, their behavior did not set well with Whiteman.

At one point in their association with Whiteman, the Rhythm Boys were scheduled to go on tour with him, but the material they were doing was not suitable for a concert-type tour. Since they had not bothered to learn anything new, Whiteman booked the trio for a separate tour on one of the vaudeville circuits instead.

But being out from under the watchful eye of their musical leader only fanned the flame of their nonconformity. The trio was supposed to do its regular singing act on the tour, but they had been exposed to so many comedy teams and had stolen so much material from these acts that their own act had changed. At one point the act consisted of an opening song, ten minutes of comedy, and a closing song. Since most of the people in the audience had bought their recordings and had come to hear them sing, their restructured act left a lot to be desired. The Rhythm Boys wavered back and forth doing the original show and their own version until the tour ended.

With the conclusion of the vaudeville tour, the Rhythm Boys returned to Whiteman's band to discover that Hollywood was stand-• ing on the threshold of a new trend—musical pictures.

In 1930, Paul Whiteman and his Orchestra went to Hollywood to make a musical talkie for Universal and he reenlisted Crosby, Barris, and Rinker.

The King of Jazz (1930, Universal Pictures) was Crosby's first feature film, but he was far from its headliner. The King of Jazz in the years during the depression was Whiteman and the lavish all-talking, all-color motion picture was especially written as a screenplay for Whiteman and his orchestra. In *The King of Jazz*, Crosby sings "Music Has Charms" over the credits, and the Rhythm Boys have four specialty numbers.

After *The King of Jazz* premiered in June 1930, the Rhythm Boys were offered more film work, some with Pathé Studios, which hired them to star in a series of two-reeler musical shorts. The first, titled *Ripstitch the Tailor*, was made in 1930 but was never released, while the second, titled *Two Plus Fours*, was released in 1930. Next came *Check and Double Check* (1930), featuring radio's favorite twosome, Amos 'n' Andy, with the Rhythm Boys appearing with Duke Ellington's Orchestra.

After the trio finished *The King of Jazz*, it was scheduled to play theater dates with Whiteman in Los Angeles, San Diego, Seattle, and Portland. In Seattle, Whiteman let Al Rinker, Harry Barris, and Bing Crosby out of their contract at their request, and the trio headed to California.

The big draw for entertainers in California was the movies and the Rhythm Boys were no different. They had a musical sequence in *Confessions of a Coed*, released in 1931, and Crosby also appeared unbilled in Douglas Fairbanks's *Reaching for the Moon* (1931).

While in California, the Rhythm Boys also played the Cocoanut Grove nightclub in Los Angeles. It was at the Cocoanut Grove that Mack Sennett, the inventor of the Keystone Kops and other silent comedy films, caught the Crosby singing act.

The late 1920s and early 1930s was a time when short subject films were still necessary to round out single feature bills at movie theaters. Sennett's gag men probably thought he had gone crazy when he suggested a series of short films with little-known Bing Crosby. But Sennett believed that audiences might respond to Crosby's unusual combination of voice and personality and signed Crosby to a series of two-reelers in 1930. At first Sennett planned to surround the singer with experienced comics and surefire comedic gags, but later he realized that Crosby, as well as being a great singer, could also handle comedy.

In addition, Crosby's looks added to the comedic genre. His ears stuck out a bit too far and that may have swayed the slapstick-minded Sennett. For Sennett, the more wingy the ears, the better for comedy.

The Sennett films were based on songs which Crosby was associated with or had recorded. Each film ran about 20 minutes. The films were shot in two- and three-day periods, with typical Sennett gagmen and funny women filling out the scenes.

The plots of these films were all pretty much the same. There might be a very social mother and daughter, and Crosby might be a band crooner with a bad reputation, someone whom the mother would not think appropriate for her daughter. Then the story would essentially be a series of gags which would wind up with a car chase or somebody falling in a fish pond. The songs were usually shot against a nightclub background or in a radio station at a microphone, and the finale would feature Crosby singing the theme song, with the mother won over to his side.

The first of these Mack Sennett shorts was *I Surrender, Dear* (1931). Some people thought that *I Surrender, Dear* was the prototype of all the "Road" pictures Crosby and Hope would make years later. Arthur Stone played opposite Crosby's flippant, happy-go-lucky, casual character, and in some ways the film is indicative of things to come.

Crosby followed *I Surrender, Dear* with *One More Chance* (1931) and *Dream House* (1931), both two-reel musical comedies.

By this time things with the Rhythm Boys at the Cocoanut Grove were pretty shaky. The trio, as usual, did not take their responsibilities seriously enough to suit management, and the club started to dock their wages. The success of Sennett's two-reelers, plus a dispute with the Cocoanut Grove's boss, brought an end to the Rhythm Boys.

Crosby then made three more two-reel shorts for Sennett: *Billboard Girl* (1931), *Blue of the Night* (1931), and *Sing, Bing, Sing* (1932).

In 1931, Crosby signed his CBS Radio contract and also appeared successfully at the Paramount Theater in New York. Armed with those honors and his success in the two-reel shorts, he signed a contract with Paramount Pictures.

The Big Broadcast of 1932 was Crosby's first film under contract, and Paramount loaded the cast with radio performers who had attained some prominence, including Burns and Allen, Kate Smith, the Mills Brothers, and Cab Calloway. The film also featured Stuart Erwin and Leila Hyams.

The story, in which Crosby portrays a happy-go-lucky crooner singing at a failing radio station operated by Burns, permitted the use of the big-name stars' various talents. In the story, Erwin, an eccentric millionaire, comes to the rescue and saves the station when he produces an all-star "big broadcast."

It was Crosby, however, whom audiences enjoyed in the movie. His singing of "Please" was the most praised moment of the film. It was apparent that Crosby was able to make the transition from radio to talking pictures, but the best that could be said of his film acting at the time was that it had "possibilities."

Still, his role in *The Big Broadcast of 1932* was enough to induce Paramount to sign him to a long-term contract. His association with Paramount would last 23 years.

In addition to the movie's success, Crosby had a hit record, "I Surrender Dear," and a national show on CBS Radio. He also was appearing live at theaters across the country. One such appearance in December 1932 brought him to a two-week engagement at the Capitol Theater in New York and the pivotal pairing with Bob Hope, who was the master of ceremonies of the Capitol show.

After his *Big Broadcast* success, in quick succession Crosby was featured in several films. The first of these was *College Humor* (1933, Paramount).

The story of *College Humor* was pretty much a cliché-ridden effort complete with the usual thrilling football game and the numerous campus sweethearts. Again, the music was more important than the story as Crosby sang "Learn to Croon" and "Down the Old Ox Road."

As in all of Crosby's early pictures, the cast was filled with members of the Paramount stock company. Richard Arlen and Jack Oakie played the straight and the comic college boys, and Mary Carlisle was the love interest. To tie in with *The Big Broadcast*, George Burns and Gracie Allen were in the picture also as Paramount continued its heavy plugging of radio names.

Crosby's next movie was *Too Much Harmony* (1933, Paramount), in which he puts together a small-town vaudeville act that takes him back to Broadway.

Too Much Harmony was inundated with experienced comedians and ad-libbers, including Jack Oakie, Skeets Gallagher, Harry Green, and Ned Sparks. Crosby found little opportunity to get a word in edgewise. It was, perhaps, this early training that prepared Bing Crosby for working with the quick-witted Bob Hope in later years.

The film also featured Judith Allen, but the Crosby songs were the main attraction. He sang "The Day You Came Along" and "Thanks" in the film.

As Crosby's film career started to take off, newspaper magnate William Randolph Hearst recognized the singer's immense appeal and hired him to bolster the sagging career of Marion Davies in a film called *Going Hollywood* (1933, Cosmopolitan-MGM). In the film, Davies plays a French teacher who falls in love with radio crooner Crosby and follows him to Hollywood and stardom. The movie also featured Fifi D'Orsay, Stuart Erwin, Ned Sparks, and Patsy Kelly.

One of the most significant aspects of the picture is that it contains Crosby's first attempt at presenting a song in dramatic fashion. After Davies has given Crosby the air for his misdeeds, he sits in a bar in Tijuana and sings "Temptation" to a glass of tequila. Through trick photography, a woman's face appears in the glass of tequila, and at the end of the song, Crosby flings the glass at the wall and staggers out of the bar and into the night. Definitely a departure for the heretofore gleeful crooner.

Hearst's investment paid off; the film restored Davies's career, made a lot of money for Hearst, and helped put Crosby on the list of the top ten money-making celebrities in 1934. In one film distributor's poll after another, Crosby was listed among the top ten movie stars, challenging the dominance of such talented actors as Will Rogers, Wallace Beery, and Marie Dressler.

The dramatic singing in *Going Hollywood* paved the way for Crosby's next chance to spread his wings a bit.

In *We're Not Dressing* (1934, Paramount), Crosby was given a chance to try more acting, as well as singing. Cast in the role of a sailor who tries to instill some sense into the domineering daughter of a millionaire, Crosby was offered more chance for characterization than he had in the usual musical.

Crosby was aided by comedienne Carole Lombard, who played the shrewish heiress. Additional comedy material came from Burns and Allen, Leon Errol, and Ethel Merman. The big song was "May I," but unlike earlier Crosby films, the songs and music were not solely responsible for the picture's success. The reviews were favorable, and Crosby was gaining some recognition as a personality, if not as an actor.

Crosby's next film, *She Loves Me Not* (1934, Paramount), was a turning point in terms of the singer's onscreen appearance. At this point in his career, the studios were still trying to pin back his somewhat protruding ears with glue. During the filming of *She Loves Me Not* the heavy lighting melted the glue and the ears flapped out. When it happened for the tenth time, Crosby reportedly gave the director an earful, "This time they're going to stay out." Eventually Paramount acquiesced, and his ears remained naturally extended throughout the rest of his career. Part of *She Loves Me Not* was shot with the ears glued back, part with them sticking out.

The film itself is a lightweight comedy about a chorus girl who seeks refuge from a pursuing gangster in the rooms of some undergraduates at Princeton. Miriam Hopkins plays the embattled chorus girl, and Crosby and Elliott Nugent play two of the undergraduates. Kitty Carlisle also was featured in the film.

Carlisle also appeared in Crosby's next film, *Here Is My Heart* (1934, Paramount), in which Crosby portrays an American millionaire who falls in love with Carlisle, a poor European princess. He poses as a waiter, learns of her problems, and eventually marries her.

Although the film was only mildly entertaining, its impact was significant for Crosby's career in several ways. First, it gave Crosby some opportunity to display his talents as a comedian, and following *We're Not Dressing* and *She Loves Me Not*, it again cinched Crosby's appearance in the box-office top ten movie stars for the year. In addition, the songs from the film, including "Love Is Just Around the Corner," "June in January," and "With Every Breath I Take," were important enough to make an impressive debut for Crosby on a new record label—Decca.

The year 1935 started with a costume picture for Crosby, his first. *Mississippi* (1935, Paramount) featured Crosby, W. C. Fields, Joan Bennett, and Gail Patrick. Crosby, who is fleeing fiancée Gail Patrick, joins a show troupe on Fields's showboat, becomes known as "The Singing Killer," then returns to marry Bennett, sister of his former fiancée.

Mississippi is not one of Crosby's better films. Overall his performance is wooden, as traces of the real Bing Crosby, rather than the character he is playing, show through. Still, the film had three good tunes: "Soon," "Down by the River," and "It's Easy to Remember."

The songs were also the saving grace in Crosby's next film, *Two for Tonight* (1935, Paramount). The film features Crosby, Joan Bennett, Mary Boland, Lynne Overman, and Thelma Todd. In this film, songwriter Crosby poses as a playwright and must turn out a complete musical comedy in a week.

The movie itself was mere nonsense, but, fortunately, *Two for Tonight* boasted five big songs: "I Wish I Were Aladdin," "From the Top of Your Head to the Tip of Your Toes," "It Takes Two to Make a Bargain," "Without a Word of Warning," and the title tune.

Paramount cranked out another "big broadcast" with *The Big Broadcast of 1936* (1935, Paramount). The film starred Jack Oakie, Burns and Allen, Wendy Barrie, and Akim Tamiroff, with specialties by Ethel Merman, Amos 'n' Andy, Mary Boland, Charlie Ruggles, Bill Robinson, and Ina Ray Hutton. Crosby did a guest appearance, singing "I Wished on the Moon."

Paramount then featured Crosby in another expensive production, *Anything Goes* (1936, Paramount). It was the movie version of Cole Porter's musical in which Crosby, Charlie Ruggles, and Ethel Merman play a group of light-fingered, light-mannered thieves who work Atlantic ocean liners. Ida Lupino appears for some of the love interest, and the songs were the Broadway musical's great hits, including "Anything Goes," "I Get a Kick Out of You," and "You're the Top."

The scene shifted from ocean liners to open skies in Crosby's next film, *Rhythm on the Range* (1936, Paramount). Crosby, a rodeo cowboy, meets debutante Frances Farmer, who is fleeing her heiress-aunt. When she decides to stay on the range, he marries her. "I'm an Old Cowhand" was one of the songs.

Crosby then made *Pennies from Heaven* (1936, Columbia), in which he delivers a letter from a condemned murderer to the victim's family and winds up marrying social worker Madge Evans and adopting 10-year-old Edith Fellows and granddad Donald Meek.

It was back to Paramount to do *Waikiki Wedding* (1937) with Shirley Ross, Bob Burns, Martha Raye, and Anthony Quinn. In this film, hotshot publicist Crosby persuades contest-winner Ross of the beauty of Hawaii. They fall in love with each other and fight off the unfriendly natives.

Right after *Waikiki Wedding* Crosby made *Double or Nothing* (1937, Paramount), in which he solves the freak problem of doubling a $5,000 inheritance in 30 days. The film also starred Mary Carlisle, Martha Raye, Andy Devine, and William Frawley.

Doctor Rhythm (1938, Major Pictures–Paramount) offered Mary Carlisle and Andy Devine again, with Beatrice Lillie carrying most of the picture's comedic moments. Louis Armstrong and his band provided some musical highlights. Crosby plays a singing bodyguard who is protecting an heiress (Carlisle) in the home of her aunt (Lillie), who is trying to prevent her niece's elopement. The film was an acceptable box-office attraction, though hardly an important Crosby film.

Also in 1938, Crosby and Hope appeared together in a short film called *Don't Hook Now* (1938, Paramount). Hope appeared as himself to help promote a Bing Crosby golf tournament.

Reportedly, film producer Herb Polesie, who had just completed the movie *Doctor Rhythm* with Crosby, had been asked by the Professional Golfers' Association to make a two-reel short of the second annual Crosby golf tournament at Rancho Santa Fe near San Diego.

The two-day, professional-amateur event, with prize money of $2,000, did not have many stars, so Polesie called Hope and suggested he help out. As the crooner sang "Tomorrow's My Lucky Day," the comedian clowned. This turned out to be an important landmark in the history of cinema—Hope and Crosby had appeared on film together for the first time.

Sing, You Sinners (1938, Paramount) was a bit of a turning point for Crosby's film career. Primarily a dramatic film, it costarred Fred MacMurray and Donald O'Connor as Crosby's younger brothers. In the film, Crosby and O'Connor form a singing act while training a horse for a race. They win the horse race and give up racing for singing so MacMurray can marry Ellen Drew. The highlight of the film was Crosby's rendition of "Small Fry."

What made the film a turning point was that Crosby found the casual acting mode his audiences loved. He played a rough sketch of himself, a lazy, happy-go-lucky, undependable, but good-hearted fellow who's mad about horses. His screen persona was taking shape.

But Crosby's career had very little help from *Paris Honeymoon* (1939, Paramount). It features millionaire cowboy Crosby seeking a honeymoon castle in France for his intended bride, Shirley Ross, but instead falling for a peasant girl (Franciska Gaal) who works in Akim Tamiroff's tavern. Additional comedy was provided by Edward Everett Horton and Ben Blue.

East Side of Heaven (1939, Universal) also did little to further the singer's film career. The film features singing cab driver Crosby, who has a child thrust upon him by its mother (Irene Hervey). He and his fiancée (Joan Blondell) reunite the child with its millionaire grandfather (C. Aubrey Smith), who sponsors a radio show with Crosby.

Things were not much better in *The Star Maker* (1939, Paramount). Crosby plays a part fashioned after the career of Gus Edwards, who had brought stars such as George Jessel, Eddie Cantor, and Walter Winchell into prominence through his children's revues. Crosby wandered through the film in checked suits, polka-dot bow ties, and derby hats. The film also starred Louise Campbell, Linda Ware, and Ned Sparks, but bears only a meager resemblance to Edward's flamboyant career. Fortunately, Crosby had good songs to save the story: "An Apple for the Teacher," "Go Fly a Kite," and "A Man and His Dream."

Crosby's next role would change the face of film comedy. In 1940, Paramount teamed him with Bob Hope and Dorothy Lamour in *Road to Singapore*.

After *Road to Singapore*, Crosby was on loan to Universal for *If I Had My Way* (1940). Crosby, as a singing steel-worker, helps an orphan (Gloria Jean) locate her ex-vaudevillian grand-uncle (Charles Winninger), who.opens a nightclub. The film was insignificant in Crosby's career, however, especially after the popularity of *Road to Singapore*.

Crosby was back to Paramount for *Rhythm on the River* (1940). This film, mainly because of the strong supporting cast, was more like the early successful Crosby pictures. It featured Mary Martin, Basil Rathbone, Oscar Levant, Charles Grapewin, William Frawley, Phyllis Kennedy, and Jeanne Cagney. The story centers on Crosby and Martin, ghost-songwriters for Rathbone. When they try to make it on their own, the audiences still believe the songs are Rathbone's.

The singer's motion picture career continued to prosper in 1941, when he teamed for the second time with Hope and Lamour in *Road to Zanzibar* (1941, Paramount).

Mary Martin was back to star with Crosby in *The Birth of the Blues* (1941, Paramount). The simple film finds singer and jazz-clarinetist Crosby forming a white band to popularize jazz in this pseudo-documentary blues anthology. Others in the cast included Brian Donlevy, Eddie Anderson, J. Carrol Naish, Carolyn Lee, Ruby Elzy, and Jack Teagarden and his Orchestra.

Crosby's greatest movie successes came during the years of World War II. The "Road" pictures were popular and Paramount was also producing a string of hits, including *Holiday Inn* (1942, Paramount).

In *Holiday Inn*, easygoing Crosby plays Jim Hardy, who quits his nightclub act with Ted Hanover (Fred Astaire) and Lila Dixon (Virginia Dale) to settle down on a Connecticut farm. When he finds himself unsuited to the life of a farmer, Crosby decides to open his place as a nightclub, but only on holidays. The film's main conflict arises when Crosby and Astaire become rivals for the affection of first their partner, Dale, and then Linda Mason (Marjorie Reynolds), the Holiday Inn's featured female entertainer. The film also starred Walter Abel and Louise Beavers.

The idea for the movie came from songwriter Irving Berlin. The premise provided Berlin with an excuse to write a song about each of the major holidays. One of the songs was "White Christmas."

Everyone involved in the picture agreed the song "White Christmas" was a catchy tune that would fit well into the movie. But many thought "Be Careful, It's My Heart," the Valentine's Day number, was going to be the big hit of the film. That was not the case. "White Christmas" is a charming and simple number, but its popularity was increased by the conditions of the time: 1942 was the first Christmas of the century during which the United States had a substantial number of troops involved in a foreign war, and the song perfectly expressed the yearning of the soldiers to be back home.

"White Christmas" won an Academy Award for Best Song in 1942. By the end of 1982, more than 143 million records of "White Christmas" had seen sold in the United States and Canada alone.

Crosby followed the successful *Holiday Inn* with the third installment of the "Road" series, *Road to Morocco* (1942, Paramount).

Because of World War II, Paramount, as well as the other studios, were developing all-star extravaganzas wrapped around a thin story line concerning servicemen. Paramount's entry was *Star Spangled Rhythm* (1942).

In this film, Betty Hutton arranges for Victor Moore, actually the gatekeeper of the studio, to appear to be the Paramount production chief in an effort to impress his son Eddie Bracken, who is in the navy. All the Paramount stars put in appearances, with Crosby singing "Old Glory."

Crosby then did another costume piece, *Dixie* (1943, Paramount), with Dorothy Lamour, Marjorie Reynolds, and Billy De Wolfe. Set in pre–Civil War New Orleans, the film claimed to be the biography of Dan Decater Emmett, composer of the title tune and many others. In reality, the movie is a fictional piece based on history which simply provided Crosby with another musical hit.

Crosby, as Emmett, marries Marjorie Reynolds. Then with pal Billy De Wolfe, he goes through some hard times, forming a minstrel troupe, doing a blackface act, and eventually writing the title song "Dixie," which became the war cry of the Confederacy.

Crosby came back strong with *Going My Way* (1944, Paramount), winning an Oscar for his portrayal of Father Chuck O'Malley, a progressive priest who helps out Father Fitzgibbon (Barry Fitzgerald) in a poor parish.

In *Going My Way*, director Leo McCarey artfully blended a series of episodes revolving around St. Dominic's parish, to which a new young priest has been sent to "get the parish in shape." In the film, Crosby is playful, modern, and psychologically oriented as the young Father O'Malley. McCarey cast the veteran Irish actor Fitzgerald as Father Fitzgibbon, the builder of the church who is astute, but just a bit behind the times. McCarey's free-and-easy handling of the two stars created a unique partnership that came across splendidly on screen. The film also featured Rise Stevens, Gene Lockhart, and Frank McHugh.

Crosby did not score as big with his next film, *Here Come the Waves* (1944, Paramount). The story is about a sailor and a musical show in which Crosby, as a prominent singer recruited by the navy, plays a part. There was some typical Hollywood trickery, with Betty Hutton playing a dual role; the cast was filled out with such Paramount players as Sonny Tufts.

The picture did not do much for Crosby's movie career, but the songs from the film included "That Old Black Magic" and "Ac-cent-chu-ate the Positive."

Paramount, still in the business of capitalizing on radio stars' appeal, put together a screen version of the popular radio show *Duffy's Tavern* (1945, Paramount). Ed Gardner, Charlie Cantor, Barry Sullivan, and Victor Moore starred in the film, and Crosby was one of the Paramount stars. Crosby sings "Swinging on a Star" with Betty Hutton, Sonny Tufts, Diana Lynn, Billy De Wolfe, Cass Daley, and Howard da Silva.

Crosby's film career in the mid–1940s brought a number of reteamings and restructuring of earlier films, all of which were successful.

In *The Bells of St. Mary's* (1945, Rainbow-RKO), Crosby reappeared as Father Chuck O'Malley, a role he first played in *Going My Way*.

The film's plot is no more original than that of *Going My Way*, and, in fact, bore some resemblances to the first story. Here the school build-ing, St. Mary's, which Sister Benedict (Ingrid Bergman) presides over, is in bad shape, physically and financially. The adversary is Henry Tra-vers, who is erecting a new building next door that the nuns fully expect to take over for their school. Crosby helps the school and arranges for a transfer to a milder climate for nun Bergman, who is an unwitting victim of tuberculosis.

Although *The Bells of St. Mary's* was not the big hit that *Going My Way* had been, it also was not a disappointment, as sequels often are. Crosby was nominated for another Best Actor Academy Award but lost to Ray Milland in *The Lost Weekend*.

Crosby scored another hit when he reteamed with Hope and Lam-our in *Road to Utopia* (1945, Paramount), and Crosby combined with Fred Astaire for a second time in *Blue Skies* (1946, Paramount).

Like *Holiday Inn*, *Blue Skies* was another Irving Berlin song cav-alcade built around a show-business story. Crosby plays a man who finds the restaurant and nightclub business irresistible. He holds off marrying Joan Caulfield as he opens one nightclub after another, each built on a different gimmick, new songs (which were old Berlin hits), and the comedy of Billy De Wolfe. When he finally marries Caulfield, he cannot keep his promise to stay with one nightclub and buys and sells several until they split. Astaire plays a dancer-turned-radio com-mentator who also competes for Caulfield.

The songs from the film included the title piece as well as "You Keep Coming Back Like a Song," "A Couple of Song and Dance Men," and "A Pretty Girl Is Like a Melody."

Crosby teamed up with Barry Fitzgerald a second time in *Welcome Stranger* (1947, Paramount), which also starred Joan Caulfield. The teaming was an obvious attempt to cash in on the box-office achieve-ment of *Going My Way*. Unfortunately, it did not meet with as much success. A young doctor (Crosby) takes over the practice of vacation-ing Fitzgerald and saves the old doctor's life with the help of a school teacher (Caulfield). Reviewers dismissed the film lightly, but audiences accepted its stars and enjoyed its songs such as "My Heart Is a Hobo" and "As Long as I'm Dreaming."

Paramount trotted out its stable of stars for *Variety Girl* (1947, Paramount), a tribute to the Variety Clubs of America. Crosby and Hope do a golfing scene together and sing "Harmony." The film also starred Mary Hatcher, Olga San Juan, William Demarest, and Frank Faylen.

Hope and Crosby teamed up again with Dorothy Lamour in the fifth film of the "Road" series, *Road to Rio* (1947, Paramount).

Crosby then made *The Emperor Waltz* (1948, Paramount). The story paralleled the love of phonograph salesman Virgil Smith (Crosby) for Johanna, Countess von Stolzenberg-Stolzenberg (Joan Fontaine), with the infatuation of Virgil's common fox terrier, Buttons, for the countess' poodle, Scheherazade. Both Virgil and Buttons suffer setbacks as a result of their mediocre standing but finally succeed in obtaining their goals.

The Emperor Waltz was followed by *A Connecticut Yankee in King Arthur's Court* (1949, Paramount) in which Crosby plays the blacksmith who, after his horse runs into a tree during a violent rainstorm, awakens to find himself as a member of King Arthur's Round Table in the days of Camelot. The film also starred Rhonda Fleming, William Bendix, and Cedric Hardwicke.

For *Top o' the Morning* (1949, Paramount), Crosby was paired a third time with Barry Fitzgerald. The film features insurance investigator Crosby posing as a singing artist who goes to Ireland to recover a stolen Blarney Stone. Crosby falls in love with Fitzgerald's daughter, Ann Blyth, but the film had none of the magic of their first film together, *Going My Way*.

The 1950s started slowly for Crosby's film career. First up was a film called *Riding High* (1950, Paramount), which was directed by Frank Capra. In this film, Crosby is engaged to Frances Gifford but leaves his job with her father to train a horse. The horse wins a big race and then dies. Crosby then falls for Gifford's younger sister, Coleen Gray, gets two new horses and begins again. The film was a remake of Frank Capra's original *Broadway Bill* (1934), which starred Warner Baxter and Myrna Loy.

The next Crosby film was *Mr. Music* (1950, Paramount), which starred Nancy Olson, Charles Coburn, Ruth Hussey, Robert Stack, and Tom Ewell. Crosby, in debt after giving up songwriting for golf, receives an advance from his producer-friend Coburn. Coburn hires Olson to make sure that Crosby keeps writing. When Coburn runs into money troubles, Crosby helps him stage a show at a college.

In 1951, Crosby made *Here Comes the Groom* (Paramount) with Jane Wyman, Franchot Tone, and Alexis Smith. In the film, Crosby, a reporter, must marry within five days to keep two war orphans. Meanwhile, old sweetheart Wyman, who has tired of waiting for Crosby to marry her, has decided to wed Tone. Crosby breaks it up in time. The duet of "In the Cool, Cool, Cool of the Evening" by Crosby and Wyman is a highlight of the film.

Wyman appears again with Crosby in *Just for You* (1952, Paramount), in which songwriter Crosby vies with his son (Robert Arthur) for Broadway star Wyman, while trying to get his daughter (Natalie Wood) into a finishing school run by Ethel Barrymore. In the end Crosby wins Wyman, his daughter enrolls in the school, and his son writes a hit song.

Things picked up again for Crosby in 1952 when he teamed with Hope and Lamour in *Road to Bali* (Paramount).

In a more dramatic role, Crosby appeared as an American journalist in the film *Little Boy Lost* (1953, Paramount), in which Crosby returns to France to find his young son who vanished during the war. The film also starred Claude Dauphin, Nicole Maurey, Christian Fourcade, Gabrielle Dorziat, and Collette Dereal.

In the mid–1950s Crosby scored substantial hits, first with a musical he wanted to do and then with a dramatic role that he didn't want.

White Christmas (1954, Paramount) was the musical, and it starred Crosby, Danny Kaye, Rosemary Clooney, Vera-Ellen, and Dean Jagger. The basis of the film was simple: Army buddies Crosby and Kaye make it in show biz, add sister act Clooney and Vera-Ellen, and help their old general Jagger promote his ski lodge.

From the beginning, *White Christmas* had some minor troubles. Financing, however, was not one of them. Paramount, Crosby, and Irving Berlin, who came out of a ten-year retirement, were sharing the bill.

The songs were not a problem either. Berlin wrote eleven new numbers for the film, nine of which were used along with such standards as "White Christmas" and "Blue Skies."

But the script and casting were other matters. The original idea was to cast Fred Astaire and Crosby together again. But reportedly Astaire saw early versions of the script and turned it down.

Studio executives then thought Donald O'Connor might step into Astaire's vacant dancing shoes, and O'Connor said he wanted to work with Crosby again (he was only 12 when they appeared together in 1938 in *Sing, You Sinners*). But supposedly O'Connor had back trouble and couldn't work.

Danny Kaye was then approached and agreed to join Crosby, provided the script was improved. It was; the movie was made, and it proved to be a huge success.

Crosby was not as enthusiastic about his next project, *The Country Girl* (1954, Paramount). In the film, musical comedy star Crosby, an alcoholic who is wallowing in self-pity, has a chance to make a comeback. His wife (Grace Kelly) and director (William Holden) help him with his return to the stage.

Crosby was against playing the role of an alcoholic actor fighting to make a comeback. Crosby felt that he was a crooner, not an actor. But director George Seaton, with whom he had made *Little Boy Lost*, pointed out to Crosby how convincing he had been in that film and persuaded him to take the role.

It paid off; Crosby was nominated for an Academy Award for Best Actor but lost to Marlon Brando in *On the Waterfront*.

In 1956, Crosby hit a landmark. *Anything Goes* (1956, Paramount) was his 50th film and his last for Paramount.

At about this time, the Hollywood star system was in demise. All the major studios, including Paramount, were competing with television and were feeling the financial drain. The studios dropped their contract players and began hiring stars on a picture-by-picture basis. Crosby made nine pictures thereafter, and none of them was with Paramount.

Anything Goes was a remake of the 1936 film with Ethel Merman and Victor Moore, but only the title and the Cole Porter songs remained. The cast and the plot differed. The film is memorable in that it reunited Crosby with Donald O'Connor. The two had last appeared together in *Sing, You Sinners* in 1938.

The flimsy plot has Crosby, as an aging matinee idol, teaming up for a Broadway show with young television star O'Connor. They find two female leads (Mitzi Gaynor and Jeanmarie) and the four of them sing and dance up a storm.

High Society (1956, MGM) was a musical version of *The Philadelphia Story*, which became a Hollywood classic in 1940 with Katharine Hepburn, Cary Grant, and James Stewart. In *High Society*, Crosby tries to win back ex-wife Grace Kelly, who is about to be remarried, and gets help from a newspaper reporter (Frank Sinatra) and a photographer (Celeste Holm). The film also featured Sidney Blackmer, John Lund, Louis Calhern, and Louis Armstrong and his band.

It was Sinatra and Crosby's first major film together, and it was the last to be made by Grace Kelly before she retired to marry Prince Rainier and become the princess of Monaco. The songs are bright and delightful. The big song that came from the movie was the ballad "True

Love," which Crosby and Kelly sang in duet. The song sold a million, earned them a gold record, and put Crosby back on the charts around the world.

Crosby then did an about-face and starred in the heavy drama *Man on Fire* (1957, MGM). Crosby again plays an alcoholic who fights to maintain custody of a son he reared after a divorce. The film also stars Inger Stevens and E. G. Marshall. The only singing done by Crosby was the title song over the opening credits.

But Crosby was singing again in *Say One for Me* (1959, 20th Century–Fox), in which he plays a priest in a show-business parish. Part of his duties entail protecting Debbie Reynolds, the daughter of an ailing friend, when she takes a job as a chorus girl. The film also featured Robert Wagner, Frank McHugh, and Ray Walston.

Crosby also sang in *Let's Make Love* (1960, 20th Century–Fox), but only as a featured player. The film starred Marilyn Monroe, Yves Montand, and Tony Randall. Crosby, Milton Berle, and Gene Kelly have roles in which they try to teach Montand to sing, tell jokes, and dance, respectively. Crosby sings "Incurably Romantic" in his lessons with Montand.

It was Crosby who was learning the lessons in his next film, *High Time* (1960, 20th Century–Fox). In the film, Crosby, a wealthy widower, returns to college to complete his education. In so doing, he falls for French teacher Nicole Maurey. The film also featured Tuesday Weld, Fabian, and Richard Beymer as Crosby's fellow students. The song "The Second Time Around" was another hit for Crosby.

Crosby was one of 35 guest stars in the film *Pepe* (1960, Columbia), in which Mexican ranch hand Cantinflas follows a prize stallion to Hollywood and meets the stars along the way. The motion picture also featured Dan Dailey, Shirley Jones, Edward G. Robinson, Ernie Kovacs, and William Demarest.

By 1962, Crosby's film career was winding down, and there was an attempt to resurrect the "Road" series at least one more time. Crosby appeared with Hope in *The Road to Hong Kong* (United Artists).

Crosby teamed up with fellow crooners Frank Sinatra, Dean Martin, and Sammy Davis, Jr., in *Robin and the Seven Hoods* (1964, Warner Bros.). Crosby plays Allen A. Dale in a Robin Hood story reset in Chicago during Prohibition. The film also starred Barbara Rush, Peter Falk, and Victor Buono.

Crosby's last feature film was *Stagecoach* (1966, 20th Century-Fox), in which he plays an alcoholic doctor in a remake of a 1939 John

Ford movie. *Stagecoach* also stars Ann-Margret, Red Buttons, Michael Connors, Alex Cord, Bob Cummings, Van Heflin, and Slim Pickens. It is a little ironic that in Crosby's last feature film he played a non-singing role.

Bing Crosby appeared in 59 feature films, and early in his career he was consistently among the top ten money-making stars in box-office polls. Because of his ability to play dramatic as well as musical roles, not only will Crosby's songs endure, but his performances will be remembered as well.

The Vaudeville Comic
Hits the Screen: The
Movies of Bob Hope

Bob Hope's onscreen character of false bravado and quick come-backs which was a hallmark of the "Road" films may have stemmed from his early training in show business. His path to the movie mar-quee followed the often demanding vaudeville circuit.

After stints as an amateur boxer and dance instructor, Hope at 19 persuaded his girlfriend, Mildred Rosequist, to become his dance part-ner. The two appeared in low-budget vaudeville shows playing in Cleveland theaters.

But Hope wanted to play bigger, out-of-town houses, and when Rosequist did not want to leave Cleveland, Hope teamed with friend Lloyd Durbin. The two developed an act in which they sang and danced in blackface. They played Cleveland's Bandbox Theatre and toured a vaudeville circuit as part of "Hurley's Jolly Follies." When Durbin became ill, Hope got George Byrne to replace him. As a spe-cialty act, the two were featured in a 1927 Broadway show called *The Sidewalks of New York* but made little impact.

The following year, Bob Hope decided to become a solo vaude-ville entertainer, and he dropped the blackface. He did, however, hire Louise Troxell to appear as his stooge on occasion.

Hope continued performing on the vaudeville circuits and even-tually played the Palace in New York. As a result of his performance there, he was signed to star in *Ballyhoo of 1932*, which opened on Broad-way in September of that year.

Still playing other engagements when he could, Hope was booked into the Capitol Theater in New York in December 1932. The engagement proved to be an important one for his career. It was during this booking that he teamed up with Bing Crosby, who was the headliner of the Capitol show.

In November 1933, Hope opened in *Roberta*, the Jerome Kern musical, playing the role of Huckleberry Haines. The cast included George Murphy, Fay Templeton, Tamara, Ray Middleton, Sydney Greenstreet, and Fred MacMurray.

Both Murphy and MacMurray would soon head for Hollywood, and studio bosses also showed an interest in Hope. Hope, however, was content where he was and satisfied with what he was doing. *Roberta* was a smash hit, and he was being sought for other Broadway shows. Hope had the best of all worlds because in between Broadway productions he could play vaudeville in the movie houses and was beginning to appear as a guest star on radio shows. He also had an offer to make some comedy shorts in New York.

Hope's first two-reeler comedy was called *Going Spanish* (1934, Educational Films). Leah Ray played opposite Hope, and his big scene came when he swallowed some Mexican jumping beans and leaped around the set like a drunken kangaroo.

The following year, the comedian was seen in the Broadway show *Say When*, with Harry Richman.

Meanwhile, the East Coast arm of Warner Bros. signed Hope to a multipicture deal. Once again they were 20-minute two-reelers, but this time the aspiring star got an opportunity to sing on celluloid, when he appeared in *Paree, Paree* (1934, Warner Bros.), the film version of Cole Porter's 1929 Broadway musical *Fifty Million Frenchmen*.

Paree, Paree was followed in quick succession by *The Old Grey Mayor* (1935, Warner Bros.), *Watch the Birdie* (1935, Warner Bros.), and *Double Exposure* (1935, Warner Bros.).

Then in December 1935, Hope opened in the 1936 *Ziegfeld Follies* on Broadway. He acted as the show's master of ceremonies, sang "I Can't Get Started with You" to a showgirl named Eve Arden, and clowned with Fanny Brice. No sooner had he left the *Ziegfeld Follies* than he starred, along with Ethel Merman and Jimmy Durante, in Cole Porter's *Red, Hot and Blue!* which opened on Broadway in October 1936.

Despite all these commitments, Hope still had time to do two more comedy short films: *Calling All Tars* (1936, Warner Bros.) and *Shop Talk* (1936, Warner Bros.).

By this time Hope was also appearing on radio regularly and, when he had some time off, could always play vaudeville houses. Because his New York career was moving along nicely, he ignored movie offers. The Broadway shows, radio, vaudeville, and the movie shorts were bringing in a weekly sum that the studios could not match. Still, the studios were interested, and several factors contributed to Hope's heading for Hollywood.

First, Mitchell Leisen and Harlan Thompson, the director and producer of a film called *The Big Broadcast of 1938* (1938, Paramount), saw Hope perform the song "I Can't Get Started with You" in the *Ziegfeld Follies* and figured he could make it in films. Second, William LeBaron, the production boss at Paramount, agreed to take a chance on Hope. And, finally, the role that Hope eventually played in his first feature film, *The Big Broadcast of 1938*, was turned down by Jack Benny. Thanks to that series of events, Hope was signed to a Paramount contract for three pictures a year.

The Big Broadcast of 1938 is a vaudeville extravaganza in which two ocean liners engage in a transatlantic race. One ocean liner is owned by T. Frothingwell (W. C. Fields), who has a wild daughter, Martha (Martha Raye). Buzz Fielding (Hope) is a radio announcer with three ex-wives seeking alimony, one of whom is Shirley Ross. In their bittersweet duet, "Thanks for the Memory," Hope and Ross engage in a sophisticated exchange about their life together.

Others in the cast included Dorothy Lamour, Lynne Overman, and Ben Blue. Hope was delighted to be working with Lamour who was an old acquaintance from his Broadway days. He first saw her singing at One Fifth Avenue, a nightspot he used to frequent, and later they met formally and became friends when she moved to the Navarre Club on Central Park South.

The song by Hope and Ross, "Thanks for the Memory," received most of the accolades, won an Oscar for Best Song, and became Hope's theme song. With a first showing that strong, Paramount thought they should pick up Hope's option for at least one more film. The man who previously had said he did not care for Hollywood was back to stay.

Hope's second feature film was *College Swing* (1938, Paramount), in which he appears with Martha Raye, Betty Grable, and George Burns and Gracie Allen, whom he had known in vaudeville. Also in the cast was Jerry Colonna, a zany trombonist with bulging eyes and a bushy mustache.

In *College Swing*, Gracie Alden (Gracie Allen) inherits a small-town college and turns it into bedlam. She reorganizes the school and imports vaudeville actors to conduct classes. Hope plays Bud Brady, a brash manager. Also in the cast were Edward Everett Horton and Ben Blue. Hope had fourth billing after Burns and Allen and Martha Raye and before Betty Grable.

The studio executives hoped that the Hope-Raye number, "How'dja Like to Love Me," would duplicate the success of "Thanks for the Memory." Although the song was well received, the chemistry wasn't there, and *College Swing* was just another star-packed vehicle that was quickly forgotten.

One thing that was not easily forgotten that year was another short Hope did called *Don't Hook Now* (1938, Paramount), in which Hope plays himself and clowns at a Bing Crosby golf tournament. The short became meaningful in film history because it marked the first time Hope and Crosby appeared together in a motion picture.

Hope's next film was an unmemorable comedy called *Give Me a Sailor* (1938, Paramount), in which he plays Jim Brewster, a navy officer. He and another navy officer (Jack Whiting) are in love with Nancy Larkin (Betty Grable). Nancy's plain sister, Letty (Martha Raye), conspires with Hope to sabotage Whiting's romance, but without success. When Letty wins a contest for the most beautiful legs, Whiting transfers his affection to her, but Letty still pursues Hope. The film had plenty of slapstick but little else. Movie executives did, however, see a versatile Hope, who could be cast as a presentable leading man or the guy who tossed around a few comedic lines.

In the meantime, the song "Thanks for the Memory" had become a big hit, and Paramount was looking for a way to cash in on it. Reportedly, Paramount had a property called *Up Pops the Devil*, and they changed the title to *Thanks for the Memory* and starred Hope and Shirley Ross in it.

In *Thanks for the Memory* (1938, Paramount), newlyweds Steve (Hope) and Anne Merrick (Shirley Ross) agree that she should go back to work as a model to support his ambitions to be an author. They run into disagreements, and their separation inspires him to finish his book. The title song is reprised, and the married couple also sings "Two Sleepy People." Still, the movie failed to impress fans and critics alike.

Also unimpressive was the film *Never Say Die* (1939, Paramount), in which Hope plays John Kidley, a multimillionaire eccentric. Kidley believes he has only a month to live when a chemist mistakenly gives him an inaccurate diagnosis. Kidley escapes marriage with an adventuress, Juno (Gale Sondergaard), and meets Mickey Hawkins (Martha

Raye), daughter of a Texas oilman who wants her to marry a prince (Alan Mowbray) instead of her sweetheart (Andy Devine). Kidley marries Mickey so she can inherit his fortune and marry her real beau. Then he discovers that he's not doomed to die and he's in love with Mickey.

Hope's career fared no better in *Some Like It Hot* (1939, Paramount). In this film, Hope plays Nicky Nelson, a fast-talking barker for a boardwalk amusement parlor. He hires drummer Gene Krupa and a small band to promote his show. He tries to book Krupa in the dance hall operated by Stephen Hanratty (Bernard Nedell), but loses the booking and his enterprise. He also loses his sweetheart, Lily Racquel (Shirley Ross), but all ends well. The film also features Una Merkel.

Some Like It Hot was Hope's fifth "B" picture in a row, and things were looking dim in terms of making a livelihood in films.

"It was the rock-bottom point in my movie career," Hope said years later. "After that one, there was no place to go but up."

Fortunately for Hope, his radio career was taking off, and the popularity of his radio show apparently did not go unnoticed by the Paramount studio brass. They upgraded Hope to "A" class pictures and filmed *The Cat and the Canary* (1939, Paramount), in which he stars with Paulette Goddard. *The Cat and the Canary* was the turning point for his movie career.

The story begins as prospective heirs to a fortune are assembled at the bayou home of an eccentric millionaire ten years after his death. The will is read, and Joyce Norman (Paulette Goddard) inherits the fortune. In short order mysterious things begin to happen, and three murders occur. Although thoroughly frightened, Wally Hampton (Hope), a mystery story buff, solves the murders and wins the girl. The film was a remake of the 1927 Universal silent film of the same title, based on the old Broadway thriller by John Willard. Others in the cast included John Beal, Douglass Montgomery, and Gale Sondergaard.

For Hope this was the first role in which he could take advantage of his ability to portray comedically the "brave coward." In Wally Hampton, Hope had found the basis of a screen character that would mold his future screen image. The reluctant heroism of Hampton, and his aptitude for quick jokes when confronted by danger, eventually became Hope's film trademarks.

If *The Cat and the Canary* turned Hope's career around, his next venture helped secure it. In 1940 he appeared with Bing Crosby and Dorothy Lamour in *Road to Singapore* (Paramount) and was in the film business for the long haul.

With Hope's star on the rise, Paramount knew enough to strike while the iron was hot. With *The Cat and the Canary* making money, it made good commercial sense to pair Hope and Paulette Goddard again. The result was *The Ghost Breakers* (1940, Paramount).

In this movie, Larry Lawrence (Hope) is a radio commentator who innocently becomes involved in a murder. Mary Carter (Goddard) saves him from the police, and he escapes in a trunk on a Cuba-bound steamer. They become romantically involved, and he offers to help her rid her spooky castle of ghosts. The film, which also features Richard Carlson, Paul Lukas, and Anthony Quinn, recaptured most of the wit and charm of Hope and Goddard's first film together. *The Ghost Breakers* was a success at the box office and received fairly good reviews.

Hope followed *The Ghost Breakers* with his second "Road" excursion, *Road to Zanzibar* (1941, Paramount).

Following *Road to Zanzibar* Hope teamed with Dorothy Lamour in *Caught in the Draft* (1941, Paramount).

In this film, Hope plays movie star Don Bolton, who enlists in the army to win the hand of Tony Fairbanks (Dorothy Lamour), daughter of the Colonel (Clarence Kolb). His agent (Lynne Overman) and chauffeur (Eddie Bracken) enlist with him. The ex-actor proves the worst of soldiers, but he and his pals end up as heroes.

The slapstick service comedy received positive reviews, and with Hope promoting the film heavily on his radio show, *Caught in the Draft* was a hit and a big moneymaker for Paramount in 1941.

Hope did not fare as well, however, with *Nothing But the Truth* (1941, Paramount). The story centers on Steve Bennett (Hope), who makes a $10,000 bet with three stockbrokers (Edward Arnold, Leif Erikson, Glenn Anders) that he can tell the truth for 24 hours. Bennett's bet money is loaned to him by Arnold's niece (Paulette Goddard). Complications arise when he attends a party aboard a lavish houseboat and is not allowed even the smallest white lie. Despite the teaming of Goddard and Hope, most critics did not think it was much of a movie. Still, the audiences seemed to like it.

Hope's next film was *Louisiana Purchase* (1941, Paramount), based on a Broadway musical of the same name with a score by Irving Berlin. The political satire centered on the life of Louisiana political boss Huey Long.

Jim Taylor (Hope) is framed by his corrupt associates of the Louisiana Purchasing Co. and becomes the target of an investigation by a U.S. senator, Oliver P. Loganberry (Victor Moore). The grafters force Taylor to frame the senator, who is lured to the restaurant of Madame Bordelaise (Irene Bordoni). Taylor's girlfriend (Vera Zorina) poses for a photograph on the senator's lap, but everything turns out all right after Taylor conducts a filibuster on the floor of the legislature. Others in the cast are Dona Drake, Raymond Walburn, Maxie Rosebloom, and Frank Albertson.

Hope was able to score another hit with *My Favorite Blonde* (1942, Paramount). With its clever screenplay by "Road" writers Don Hartman and Frank Butler, *My Favorite Blonde* turned out to be a tremendous box-office success and one of Hope's better pictures. The film also began something else: a series of its own. Hope made two more "My Favorites"—*Brunette* and *Spy*—and a string of films in which he plays a romantic lead.

In *My Favorite Blonde*, Hope plays Larry Haines, a small-time variety show performer with a trained penguin. Karen Bentley (Madeleine Carroll) seeks his help in carrying secret instructions from the British government to the Lockheed factory in Los Angeles. Haines believes he is dealing with a beautiful but dizzy blonde, but soon he is entangled with Nazi agents (Gale Sondergaard and George Zucco).

Hope followed this hit with yet another, scoring big with the third entry of the "Road" series, *Road to Morocco* (1942, Paramount).

Right after *Road to Morocco*, Hope appeared in *Star Spangled Rhythm* (1942, Paramount), a musical extravaganza to help boost the morale of the men at war.

In *Star Spangled Rhythm*, a young sailor (Eddie Bracken) arrives in Hollywood to visit his father (Victor Moore), a studio gateman who has told his son he runs the place. The studio switchboard operator (Betty Hutton) has been corresponding with the sailor and helps maintain the deception. Hope appears as master of ceremonies and takes part in some skits as all the Paramount stars put in appearances in the film.

For his next picture, Hope left Paramount and was on loan to Samuel Goldwyn for *They Got Me Covered* (1943, RKO Radio).

In the film, Hope plays Robert Kittredge, a foreign correspondent who is fired by his news agency. He tries to regain his job by exposing saboteurs he has learned about through a Romanian fugitive (John Abbott). Kittredge and his fiancée, Christina Hill (Dorothy Lamour), become entangled with a spy ring, and after many mishaps he captures the spies single-handedly. The cast also features Lenore Aubert and Otto Preminger.

They Got Me Covered was not a great picture, but by this time Hope was such a strong box-office draw that it really didn't matter.

Hope was back at Paramount for his next film, *Let's Face It* (1943, Paramount), but it too was not that great an entry. The story centers on Jerry Walker (Hope) and his soldier buddies Barney Hilliard (Dave Willock) and Frankie Burns (Cully Richards), who are hired to act as gigolos. Three wives (Eve Arden, ZaSu Pitts, and Phyllis Povah) are seeking revenge on their philandering husbands, and complications arise when the soldiers' sweeties (Betty Hutton, Dona Drake, and Marjorie Weaver) discover the reluctant love-making. The film did not do much for anyone's career.

Hope fared only a little better in the costume piece *The Princess and the Pirate* (1944, RKO Radio). In this film, magician Sylvester the Great (Hope) sails for America after a less than successful career as an actor in eighteenth-century England. Also on the boat is Princess Margaret (Virginia Mayo), who is fleeing incognito because her father won't allow her to marry a commoner. Their ship is sacked by pirates led by the Hook (Victor McLaglen), but a half-witted buccaneer (Walter Brennan) helps the pair to escape to a pirate stronghold island and a raucous time ensues. Walter Slezak is also in the cast.

Fortunately for Hope's career, he returned to Paramount for *Road to Utopia* (1945, Paramount).

After *Road to Utopia* Hope appeared in the costume farce *Monsieur Beaucaire* (1946, Paramount), a remake of the 1924 silent film starring Rudolph Valentino.

In the film, Monsieur Beaucaire (Hope) is barber to the French court and in love with the beautiful scullery maid Mimi (Joan Caulfield). He gets in trouble with the king (Reginald Owen) and everyone else except the Duc de Chandre (Patric Knowles), who rescues him from the guillotine and takes him to the Spanish court. Beaucaire poses as a nobleman and gets in more trouble. The film also features Marjorie Reynolds and Cecil Kellaway.

Hope's second "My Favorite" film was *My Favorite Brunette* (1947, Paramount). This time Hope plays Ronnie Jackson, who relates in flashback how he earned a living as a baby photographer though he yearned to be like the private detective next door. His ambitions entangle him with mystery woman Carlotta Montay (Dorothy Lamour), who holds a map which pinpoints the location of valuable mineral deposits. Jackson tangles with crooks Charles Dingle, Peter Lorre, and Lon Chaney, Jr., who scramble to reach the mineral deposits first. Jackson gets framed for the murder of a government official (Reginald Denny) but is exonerated at the last moment.

Hope teamed up with Crosby for a film in 1947, but it was not a "Road" picture. The film *Variety Girl* (1947, Paramount) centered on Catherine Brown (Mary Hatcher), the first foundling of the show business charity organization, Variety Clubs. Brown goes to Hollywood for a screen test and meets Amber LaVonne (Olga San Juan). Both girls come in contact with just about every star on the Paramount lot in 1947. Hope and Crosby appear in a song-and-dance number, "Harmony." The film also features William Demarest and Frank Faylen.

In 1947, Hope made *Where There's Life* (Paramount), but there was not much life in the plot of the film. In this simple story, the king of a mythical kingdom confesses on his deathbed that he sired a son who now lives in America. The son turns out to be Michael Valentine (Hope), an all-night disc jockey for a dog food company. A delegation, which includes a female army general (Signe Hasso), goes to New York to return Valentine to his throne. Rival political factions aim to liquidate the new king as New York cop Victor O'Brien (William Bendix) gets involved in the rescue.

Hope next went on the "Road" with his fifth feature with Crosby and Lamour, *Road to Rio* (1947, Paramount).

The successful *Road to Rio* was followed by another triumph with *The Paleface* (1948, Paramount), which turned out to be Hope's biggest box-office film. The film was successful in part because the song "Buttons and Bows" from the movie was released before the picture and became very popular. The song won the Oscar for the best movie song of 1948.

In the film, Painless Peter Potter (Hope) is a correspondence-school dentist who takes his trade to the Wild West. He meets up with Calamity Jane (Jane Russell), who is seeking the culprit who is selling arms to the Indians. If she succeeds in tracking down the villains, she will be pardoned for earlier crimes she has committed. She marries the dentist to avoid suspicion but later falls for him. Potter becomes an unwilling hero when the culprits are captured. The bright comedy also features Robert Armstrong and Iris Adrian.

Russell was not that great an actress, and the script wasn't much of a script, but *The Paleface* emerged as a smash hit as Hope played his cowardly braggart role to perfection.

Hope was almost as successful in his next film, *Sorrowful Jones* (1949, Paramount), as the audience gave it an enthusiastic response and so did the critics. But the film is also memorable for two other reasons: it was the first semiserious role that Hope played and it was his first movie with Lucille Ball.

In the film, which was based on the Shirley Temple movie *Little Miss Marker*, bookie Sorrowful Jones (Hope) accepts a bet from a man who leaves his daughter Martha Jane (Mary Jane Saunders) as collateral and fails to return. Sorrowful is forced to become a foster father when he learns the real father has been killed by gangsters over a racehorse fix. Nightclub singer Gladys O'Neil (Lucille Ball) helps Sorrowful take care of the little girl. Martha Jane is hurt in an accident, and her recovery depends on seeing her beloved horse which, of course, she does. The film also features William Demarest and Bruce Cabot.

But not all Hope films were coming up winners, however. *The Great Lover* (1949, Paramount) was a great disappointment.

In *The Great Lover* Hope plays Freddie Hunter, a reporter who has been sent to Europe as counselor of a group of boy rangers. On the ocean liner, he becomes involved with a card sharp (Roland Young), a beautiful duchess (Rhonda Fleming), and her impoverished father, Grand Duke Maximilian (Roland Culver). Detective Higgins (Jim Backus) is killed by the card sharp to cover up his dealings. Hunter is implicated as an accomplice and must clear himself with his youthful charges. It was not much of a movie.

Fancy Pants (1950, Paramount), however, was a little better. In this film, Agatha Flood (Lucille Ball), newly rich from New Mexico, travels across Europe to absorb the culture. She returns home with an English actor-turned-butler, Humphrey (Hope), whom the frontier townsmen take for an earl. Her father (Jack Kirkwood) and sweetheart (Bruce Cabot) try to get rid of Humphrey through various means.

Fancy Pants was generally well received by the critics and the reviews were reflected in the box-office returns. It was another semi-hit for Hope.

Another successful film for Hope was *The Lemon Drop Kid* (1951, Paramount). In this Damon Runyon story, the Lemon Drop Kid (Hope) is a racetrack tout who gets in trouble with bad tips at a Florida track. Moose Moran (Fred Clark) gives him until Christmas to make up a $10,000 error. Unable to raise the money in New York, the Kid opens an old folks' home as a ruse to license bogus Santa Clauses on the city streets. Charley (Lloyd Nolan) muscles in on the racket, but the Kid manages to escape the heat and land both Moose and Charley in jail. The film also features Marilyn Maxwell and Jane Darwell.

Hope followed *The Lemon Drop Kid* with another "My Favorite" film. This time it was *My Favorite Spy* (1951, Paramount) in which government agents spot a second-rate burlesque comic named Peanuts White (Hope), who bears a remarkable resemblance to a notorious spy. When the spy is wounded, Peanuts is persuaded to impersonate him on a mission to Tangier. He encounters a counterspy, Lili Danielle (Hedy Lamarr), and wins her over to his side. He has less fortune with superspy Brubaker (Francis L. Sullivan) and his murderous cohorts, but Peanuts finally beats them at their own game.

Sequels are always appealing to studio executives, and as far as sequels go, *Son of Paleface* (1952, Paramount) was not too bad.

In this follow up to *Paleface*, the son of the late pioneer dentist, Painless Potter, is a callow Harvard graduate called Junior (Hope). He goes West to claim his inheritance and becomes involved in the efforts of Roy Rogers (playing himself) to track down a bandit who has been looting gold shipments. Suspicions center on Mike (Jane Russell), who runs the Dirty Shame saloon. The speculation proves correct, and after a lengthy chase, Junior gets the girl.

Son of Paleface opened to reviews astonishingly good for a sequel. Some reviews were even better than had been accorded the original from which it was derived.

In 1952, Hope scored another "Road" hit with *Road to Bali* (Paramount), but followed it with a weak film called *Off Limits* (1953, Paramount).

In *Off Limits*, Wally Hogan (Hope) is the manager of prizefighter Bullets Bradley (Stanley Clements), who is drafted into the army. Wally's partners persuade him to enlist to look after his boy, then the partners cut him out of Bradley's fight profits. Wally develops a new fighter, Herbert Tuttle (Mickey Rooney), to win the championship. Wally's enthusiasm is upset by his affection for Tuttle's aunt (Marilyn Maxwell), who hates fighting. In the end, Tuttle wins the title by some offbeat tactics. The film also features Eddie Mayehoff and Jack Dempsey. It was not one of Hope's better films.

Hope's motion picture career was not helped by *Here Come the Girls* (1953, Paramount) either. Stanley Snodgrass (Hope) is an awkward chorus boy with a knack for breaking up production numbers. After being fired by an irate producer (Fred Clark), he seems destined to seek regular employment. Surprisingly, he is suddenly thrown into the lead of a musical. He learns later that the reason for his quick star status is simple: Jack the Slasher (Robert Strauss) wants to murder the real star (Tony Martin) because of his romance with Irene Bailey (Arlene Dahl). Stanley forsakes his own girlfriend (Rosemary Clooney) to pursue Irene and thus become a clay pigeon. Although the film ends happily, it did nothing for Hope's movie career.

Another film that failed to enhance Hope's film profession was *Casanova's Big Night* (1954, Paramount). Hope plays Pippo Poppolino, a tailor's assistant who poses as Casanova. The duchess of Castelbello (Hope Emerson) hires him to test the love of Elena (Audrey Dalton), who is engaged to the duchess's son (Robert Hutton). Pippo is aided in his quest by Casanova's valet (Basil Rathbone) and grocer (Joan Fontaine), who hopes to collect on Casanova's grocery bills. All three become ensnared in the intrigue of the Doge (Arnold Moss). *Casanova's Big Night* was memorable only for its all-star cast, which also included John Carradine, Lon Chaney, Jr., and a young Raymond Burr.

Despite several weak entries in his movie career in the early 1950s, Hope turned things around in 1955 with *The Seven Little Foys* (Paramount). For the first time, he played a real-life character, and although there was plenty of comedy, he was making his debut as a dramatic actor.

The film is about vaudevillian Eddie Foy (Hope), who swears he will always remain single but falls for a ballet beauty, Madeleine Morando (Milly Vitale). They have seven children, but he is not much of a husband and father, pursuing his career most of the time. When his wife dies, Eddie is forced to take over the family and he trains his kids to join his vaudeville act. The film also features James Cagney as George M. Cohan, and his dance sequence with Hope during a banquet scene in the picture is still considered one of the finer moments in film history.

Hope wanted to capture Eddie Foy's character as fully as possible and reportedly studied everything he could find about Foy's life, including some silent movies he had made. As a serious actor, Hope was successful in reaching Foy's darker side, including the self-indulgence and the unpleasant attitude Foy seems to have had about human relationships. For the most part, the critics liked what they saw and complimented Hope for not playing Hope onscreen, but "acting and doing a commendable job."

With such a successful outing as *The Seven Little Foys* it would be difficult to follow it with another hit. *That Certain Feeling* (1956, Paramount) was definitely not a hit.

That Certain Feeling featured Hope as Francis X. Digman, a cartoonist whose life is in ruins because he gets sick to his stomach every time he gets angry. This failing has destroyed his marriage to Dunreath (Eva Marie Saint) and made him seem like a coward. Meanwhile, Dunreath has been working as a secretary to Larry Larkin (George Sanders), a successful comic strip artist. Larkin hires Digman as an assistant, and Digman tries to head off his former wife's marriage to the rival. Neither Hope nor Eva Marie Saint was considered to have given an all-out performance in the film, and most of the critics agreed that Hope was miscast as the cartoonist and that Eva Marie Saint didn't handle comedy very well.

That Certain Feeling heralded the end of Hope's 17-year association with Paramount. The studio system was coming to an end, and actors were making films for whoever wanted them. In Hope's case, he would still make some for Paramount, but his first stop was Metro-Goldwyn-Mayer and *The Iron Petticoat* (1956).

A Cold War political satire, *The Iron Petticoat* features Hope playing Major Chuck Lockwood in the psychological warfare division of the U.S. Army based in Germany. A female Russian pilot (Katharine Hepburn) lands her plane in the American zone of Germany and is handed over to Lockwood for conversion to democracy. He falls for her and becomes involved in Russian attempts to liquidate them both. The film was a mishmash and a box-office dud. Even the two star names of Hope and Hepburn could not save it.

After his success with playing a real-life character in *The Seven Little Foys*, Hope got the chance to play his second screen biographical role, as Mayor James Walker in *Beau James* (1957, Paramount).

Walker, a one-time songwriter and occasional entertainer, became New York's most renowned politician in the roaring twenties. In the film, Walker finds his political career in jeopardy because of his love for an actress, Betty Compton (Vera Miles). Walker, a Catholic who already has a wife (Alexis Smith), tries to run the city fairly but falls into a financial arrangement that discredits and defeats him. This movie also features Paul Douglas, Darren McGavin, and Jimmy Durante.

In *Beau James*, Hope again was given a complex character and a chance to combine comedy with drama. The role netted Hope many accolades.

But honors were hard to come by in *Paris Holiday* (1958, United Artists). In this film, Hope plays Robert Leslie Hunter, an American entertainer who goes to France to acquire a French play for his next vehicle. He meets up with Fernydel (Fernandel), a Frenchman who plays Cupid for Hunter, and Ann McCall (Martha Hyer), who is on her way to the American Embassy. Everyone becomes involved with Zara (Anita Ekberg), a beautiful spy. Hunter learns that the comedy he plans to acquire is in reality an exposé of a French counterfeiting ring, and he and the others become enmeshed in a lengthy chase with the culprits. *Paris Holiday* was a fiasco financially and artistically.

Only slightly better was *Alias Jesse James* (1959, United Artists). In the flick, Milford Farnsworth (Hope) is a Coney Island insurance salesman sent West to cancel an insurance policy on the life of Jesse James (Wendell Corey), who is considered a poor risk. James's girl-friend, Cora Lee Collins (Rhonda Fleming), is the beneficiary of the policy, and Farnsworth falls for her. James gets the idea of having the insurance man pose as himself and then be killed as Jesse James, but Farnsworth discovers the plot and ends up capturing the James gang. There are some bright moments, but the film was not as endearing as earlier Hope Western adventures.

Hope scored another hit with *The Facts of Life* (1960, United Artists), mainly because he was teamed with Lucille Ball. It was their third film together.

The story concerns two suburban Californians (Hope and Ball) who fall in love and attempt to have an adulterous affair. In the end, weary of the frustrations that befall them, the would-be illicit lovers return to their mates and eternal boredom.

The Facts of Life was widely acclaimed as one of Hope's most suc-cessful films, and his performance was highly praised. For the most part, critics adored the film, and it did very well at the box office. Some crit-ics considered it the best film of Hope's career.

The casting may have been perfect for *The Facts of Life*, but that was hardly the case for *Bachelor in Paradise* (1961, MGM). The film fea-tures Hope as Adam J. Niles, a best-selling author who runs into trou-ble with the government when an aide disappears without paying Niles's income tax. His publisher advises him to write a book on how America lives, so the author moves into Paradise Hill Village, disguises himself, and begins doing research among the housewives. He falls for Rosemary Howard (Lana Turner), who works in the development office. Local husbands led by Thomas Jynson (Don Porter) become suspicious of Niles and try to run him out of the neighborhood. The film also features Janis Paige, Jim Hutton, and Paula Prentiss.

The main problem in casting was Lana Turner. Although sexy, she was not Lucille Ball, and Hope and Turner did not work that well together onscreen. The script was also not up to par. The result was a film that Hope wasn't particularly proud of and that the critics were indifferent about at best.

Bachelor in Paradise was followed by *The Road to Hong Kong* (1962, United Artists), which marked the beginning of the end of Hope's glittering screen career. By 1962, Hope's two-decade domination of the leading money earners at the cinema box office was coming to a conclusion. In the following ten years, he would make only nine more major movies.

Critic's Choice (1963, Warner Brothers) teamed Hope with Lucille Ball again, but not even that could help the weak film. The story centers on Broadway critic Parker Ballentine (Hope), who is faced with the crisis of reviewing a play written by his wife Angela (Lucille Ball). He overcomes the dilemma by showing up at the premiere drunk and creating a disturbance. Then he writes a devastating review, which causes havoc in his marriage. The movie also features Marilyn Maxwell, Rip Torn, and Jessie Royce Landis.

Another weak entry in the Hope film career was *Call Me Bwana* (1963, United Artists). This tired effort features Hope as Matt Merriwether, a bogus explorer who has written books of African adventures based on the exploits of his uncle. An American moon-probe capsule lands in Africa, and the government enlists Merriwether to find the capsule before enemy nations get to it. He reluctantly goes to Africa, accompanied by a secret agent, Frederica Larsen (Edie Adams). They encounter an enemy spy, Luba (Anita Ekberg), and fellow agent Ezra Mungo (Lionel Jeffries), who poses as a missionary. The film received a poor reception by fans and critics alike.

Also receiving a poor reception was *A Global Affair* (1964, MGM). Frank Larrimore (Hope) is a United Nations department head who discovers a baby in the UN building. Since the UN building is international territory, the abandoned child becomes the center of politically motivated competition among various countries for the right to adopt the youngster. Ladies of various nationalities seek to persuade Larrimore to favor their countries, but he decides to adopt the baby himself as "the world's first truly international citizen." The film also stars Michele Mercier, Elga Andersen, and Yvonne DeCarlo.

With a series of failures on his hands, Hope and his writers tried a different attack with *I'll Take Sweden* (1965, United Artists). Hope's writers injected some blue humor into the script, and the result was disastrous.

In the film, Bob Holcomb (Hope) is a widower with a daughter named JoJo (Tuesday Weld). Holcomb doesn't approve of her friends, especially beau Kenny Klinger (Frankie Avalon), who rides a motorcycle. Hoping to get JoJo away from Klinger, Holcomb arranges to be transferred to Sweden, where JoJo falls for a suave playboy (Jeremy Slate) and Holcomb becomes involved with an interior decorator (Dina Merrill). The alarmed father brings Klinger from California in an attempt to break up the liaison with the playboy.

The critics were not pleased with the double-entendre lines in the film. In the *New York Times*, A. H. Weiler wrote: "*I'll Take Sweden* is altogether unworthy of a beloved sunshine man who has cheered millions."

Hope did not fare much better with his next flick, *Boy, Did I Get a Wrong Number* (1966, United Artists). Hope's new leading lady in this and two subsequent films was Phyllis Diller.

In *Boy, Did I Get a Wrong Number*, Hope plays real estate man Tom Meade, who dials a wrong number and becomes connected with a glamorous film star, Didi (Elke Sommer). She has taken refuge is his Oregon town to escape her boyfriend, film director Pepe (Cesare Danova). When her car is found in a lake, Meade is accused of her murder, and his problems are compounded by his wacky maid (Phyllis Diller). There was not much in this film that was worth seeing.

The next Hope-Diller feature was *Eight on the Lam* (1967, United Artists). The story features widower Henry Dimsdale (Hope) as a bank teller with seven children and an unpaid housekeeper, Golda (Phyllis Diller). Dimsdale finds $10,000 in a parking lot and buys a new car. A $50,000 embezzlement is discovered in his books at the bank, and Dimsdale is persuaded by a friend to flee until he can find a way to clear himself. He takes off with the seven kids and their dog, pursued by police and Detective Jasper Lynch (Jonathan Winters), boyfriend of Golda. The film also stars Shirley Eaton and Jill St. John. It was obvious from the reviews that Hope's film career was approaching its end.

Hope's last film with Phyllis Diller was *The Private Navy of Sgt. O'Farrell* (1968, United Artists). The film is set on a South Pacific island which has been bypassed by the war. Concerned over the troops' morale, Master Sgt. Dan O'Farrell (Hope) is seeking a cargo ship loaded with beer which has been torpedoed. During his mission he encounters a wacky nurse (Phyllis Diller), a Japanese soldier (Mako), and a former sweetheart (Gina Lollobrigida), who has been shipwrecked. He also manages to capture a Japanese submarine. The movie also features Jeffrey Hunter. The film did nothing to further anyone's career, however.

In an effort to keep current, Hope did a generation gap comedy in 1971 called *How to Commit Marriage* (Cinerama).

Frank and Elaine Benson (Hope, Jane Wyman) have decided on a divorce, but daughter Nancy (Joanna Cameron) comes home from college to announce that she is marrying David Poe (Tim Matheson), the son of a cynical rock-show promoter, Oliver Poe (Jackie Gleason). When Nancy finds out about her parents' split, she decides to skip marriage and move in with David. The pair join a rock group, and she becomes pregnant and puts the baby up for adoption. The grandparents adopt the child, complicating their own romances with other partners. Also in the cast are Maureen Arthur and Leslie Nielsen.

The film focused on the changing morality in the 1960s in general, with emphasis on sex. It relied heavily on the Hope-Gleason golf rivalry and used insult humor for laughs. The picture turned out to be the last Hope film to make a profit at the box office.

Hope's film career ended with *Cancel My Reservation* (1972, Warner Bros.).

The story centers on Dan and Sheila Bartlett (Hope and Eva Marie Saint) who have a daytime television show in New York. They come into conflict over women's rights, and a doctor advises Dan to take some time off by himself. He goes off to his ranch in Arizona and becomes implicated when the body of a dead Native American girl is found in his car. In trying to exonerate himself, Dan becomes more deeply involved in an intrigue revolving around a wealthy landowner (Ralph Bellamy) and the Native Americans. Also in the cast are Forrest Tucker, Keenan Wynn, and Doodles Weaver.

Unfortunately, *Cancel My Reservation* was a sad end to an otherwise brilliant film career for Bob Hope, who made 54 feature films and early in his career was consistently among the top draws at the box office. The venerable comedian brought hours of laughter to moviegoers young and old and made some classic films that will long be remembered.

Have Sarong, Will Travel: The Movies of Dorothy Lamour

Although the image of Dorothy Lamour cavorting about in a sexy sarong was enhanced by her roles in the "Road" series, it did not originate with those raucous films. The alluring sarong first appeared in Lamour's film debut, *The Jungle Princess*, in 1936. Her image as a cloth-draped enchantress was advanced in such films as *The Hurricane* (1937) and *Her Jungle Love* (1938). By the time *Road to Singapore* began filming, her appearance as a sarong-clad beauty was almost a foregone conclusion.

Dorothy Lamour was a nightclub singer in New York and a vocalist on an NBC radio show called *The Dreamer of Songs* in the early 1930s. Lamour went with the show when it migrated to the West Coast and performed in nightclubs where several movie studio bosses caught her act. Eventually, Paramount executives asked her to do a screen test and then signed her to a contract.

The top brass at Paramount told Lamour that they had been having difficulty casting the exotic lead for a tropical-romance story called *The Jungle Princess*. They reportedly had tested more than 250 women for the role but could not find the right person, so they shelved the picture. Now, after seeing her screen test, the execs thought the part was perfect for Lamour.

As the lead in the film, Lamour naturally thought she would be decked out in beautiful gowns with glamorous accessories. She was more than a little disappointed to learn that all the material being draped around her was only for a sarong.

The simple plot of *The Jungle Princess* (1936, Paramount) has Ray Milland, as a British hunter, being injured on an island, and then rescued by an innocent native girl (Lamour) and her pets, a tiger and a chimpanzee. Milland teaches the innocent native English and in the process falls in love with her. Meanwhile, Akim Tamiroff causes a stir among the local savages by claiming that Lamour is a voodoo girl. Milland eventually chooses Lamour over his impolite fiancée, Molly Lamount.

Paramount had designated *The Jungle Princess* as a low-budget film, but audience reaction at early screenings told them differently. *Variety* said, "[Lamour] lands powerfully in spite of the highly improbable story which makes her a female Tarzan and calls upon her to play a rather difficult role." The studio quickly altered its sales campaign and gave the movie a bigger buildup.

In one fell swoop, Lamour had found a place in the uncertain but lucrative world of motion pictures. Her sensual beauty and effortless singing style had caught the public's attention. She was on her way.

In 1937, Lamour made *Swing High, Swing Low* for Paramount. Trumpet player Fred MacMurray marries nightclub singer Carole Lombard in Panama. MacMurray takes a better job in New York, forgets Lombard, and starts to drink heavily. Lombard divorces him but later returns to help him redeem himself. Lamour is fifth-billed as Anita Alvarez, a dancer who comes between MacMurray and Lombard.

Lamour then made *Last Train from Madrid* (1937, Paramount), a "B" melodrama which was touted as being the first American feature film to deal with the Spanish Civil War. As with many of today's "disaster" epics, *Last Train from Madrid* featured several "names" including Lew Ayres, Gilbert Roland, and Anthony Quinn, all thrown together in tragedy and turmoil. Lamour plays Roland's mysterious sweetheart.

Lamour's next film, *High, Wide and Handsome* (1937, Paramount), was a $1.9 million saga of Pennsylvania oil-well pioneering in the 1850s featuring Randolph Scott, Irene Dunne, and Alan Hale. Scott and his group of oil pipeline workers lay pipe themselves in order to prevent corrupt railroad president Hale from monopolizing the industry. Dunne, a circus performer who weds Scott and then leaves him, received the most acclaim for her work. Lamour is third-billed as Molly, a honky-tonk torch singer and Hale's mistress.

After screening *The Jungle Princess*, independent producer Samuel Goldwyn was astute enough to realize that Lamour had significant box-office potential. He traded the services of Joel McCrea to Paramount for its *Union Pacific* in return for borrowing Lamour for Goldwyn's new production, *The Hurricane* (1937, United Artists), which John Ford was directing.

The Hurricane is set on the Samoan island of Manukura, and Lamour appears as Marama, daughter of the native chief. She weds sailor Jon Hall, who always seems to be in trouble with the British authorities. Others in the film included Raymond Massey, Thomas Mitchell, Mary Astor, and John Carradine. When the title storm rips the island apart, Hall appears in time to save those in danger. For his efforts, the governor (Massey) pardons Hall, who then paddles off into the sunset with Lamour and their child.

The picture was a popular success mainly because of the special effects of the magnificent hurricane, which was estimated to cost the studio $400,000 to produce. Most of Lamour's reviews centered on her physical attributes, but this notable production made her well known to both the industry and to the moviegoing public.

Lamour's fifth and final film of the year was *Thrill of a Lifetime* (1937, Paramount). This contrived musical is set in a summer resort camp and features Betty Grable, Judy Canova, Ben Blue, Leif Erickson, Larry Crabbe, Johnny Downs, and the Yacht Club Boys (with whom Lamour worked in nightclubs in New York). Lamour appears in a cameo playing herself and singing the title tune.

Lamour next joined the studio's newest vaudeville extravaganza in *The Big Broadcast of 1938* (1938, Paramount). The picture is more noteworthy as Bob Hope's feature film debut, in which he and Shirley Ross sing the Oscar-winning "Thanks for the Memory," which became Hope's theme song. *The Big Broadcast of 1938* also features W. C. Fields in a dual role and the slapstick shenanigans of Martha Raye. As for Lamour, her duties in the film were to hold fiancé Hope at bay while inciting romantic interest in Leif Erickson.

Noting a good thing when they saw it, Paramount executives followed Goldwyn's lead and again teamed Lamour with Ray Milland in the Technicolor *Her Jungle Love* (1938, Paramount). As Tura, the sarong-clad child of the jungle, Lamour finds British aviator Milland when his plane crashes on her Malayan isle. Lynne Overman is Milland's copilot, Dorothy Howe is Milland's erstwhile fiancée, and J. Carrol Naish is the native villain. Lamour sang a few songs but failed to impress the critics.

Lamour was again teamed with Milland in *Tropic Holiday* (1938, Paramount), set in Rosita, Mexico. This time Milland is a screenwriter seeking inspiration in a foreign country, and Martha Raye plays his sassy secretary. Lamour plays a love-hungry senorita, but although she had several songs, Mexican performer Elvia Rios stole the show.

Originally Carole Lombard had been scheduled for the lead in *Spawn of the North* (1938, Paramount), but by the time director Henry Hathaway had completed outdoor location shooting, Lombard had taken ill, so Lamour was hastily substituted into the part.

This action film is set in the 1890s and centers on the salmon-canning industry. John Barrymore plays the local newspaper editor, Louise Platt plays his daughter, Henry Fonda plays the owner of the cannery, and George Raft plays a schemer. Lamour is billed third as Nicky Duval, a French Canadian fishing camp girl in love with Raft.

Lamour had top billing in *St. Louis Blues* (1939, Paramount) which was nothing more than a variation on the *Show Boat* theme, with less admirable results. Lamour portrays a Broadway musical comedy star who leaves New York to avoid playing the same type of role over and over again. She meets showboat captain Lloyd Nolan, who wants to star her in his new revue. William Frawley, as a competing carnival owner, almost prevents the big show from going on. Lamour sang several songs in the film, but more noteworthy in the singing department were Tito Guizar and Maxwell Sullivan.

Man About Town (1939, Paramount), a Jack Benny musical-comedy vehicle, was to feature Betty Grable opposite the comedian. When Grable became ill, however, Lamour again filled in. The movie features producer Benny in London with his new show and dating Binnie Barnes in order to make his girlfriend (Lamour) jealous. Lamour sang with Phil Harris and performed a solo number.

Lamour went dramatic in *Disputed Passage* (1939, Paramount), in which John Howard is cast as the refined medical student of surgeon Akim Tamiroff. Lamour appears as Audrey Hilton, who has been raised by Chinese foster parents. When Howard's infatuation with Lamour seriously jeopardizes his studies, Tamiroff convinces Lamour to return to China. Howard later turns up in China and is injured in a bombing raid. Tamiroff arrives to operate, and Lamour reappears to offer Howard the faith necessary for recovery. This weak drama went nowhere at the box office.

On loan to Twentieth Century–Fox, Lamour costarred with Tyrone Power in the gangster melodrama *Johnny Apollo* (1940), directed by Henry Hathaway. Power, who plays the college-bred son of crooked stockbroker Edward Arnold, turns dishonest and becomes the right-hand man of racketeer Lloyd Nolan when Arnold is sent to prison for embezzlement. Lamour plays Lucky Dubarry, Nolan's girlfriend, who becomes interested in Power. Still, she has time to warble a few songs.

In *Typhoon* (1940, Paramount), Dorothy Lamour plays Dea, a castaway since childhood who grows up on an island off Dutch Guiana. The film has Robert Preston being coerced by Lynne Overman to help search for pearls, and when the crew mutinies, Preston and Overman are left on Lamour's isle. The natives get stirred up by J. Carrol Naish, who plots to destroy the visiting white men, but a typhoon conveniently kills the evil ones and saves the good people. Lamour sported an abbreviated sarong in this picture and hung around with a chimpanzee. She had only one song in the film.

The late 1930s and early 1940s brought rumblings of another world war and audiences sought to escape the harsh reality of life with films that were a little more entertaining. At that time there were "screwball comedies" and "social comedies," but Paramount wanted a new idea. At about the same time, Lamour found that she had reached a certain level of stardom singing beautiful songs in her sarong, and she too wanted to do something different. Lamour and the studio got their wish with *Road to Singapore* (1940, Paramount).

Lamour always wanted to stretch herself as an actress and tried to do so in *Moon Over Burma* (1940, Paramount). Unfortunately, *Moon Over Burma* was a mediocre jungle-triangle romance at best. Robert Preston and Preston Foster operate a lumber camp for blind owner Albert Basserman. Foster falls for American entertainer Lamour, and a brutal log jam and fierce forest fire transpire before the standard wrap-up of the story.

On loan again to Twentieth Century–Fox, Lamour costarred with Henry Fonda in *Chad Hanna* (1940), a Technicolor saga of circus life in 1841 New York. Lamour plays Albany Yates, the bareback rider whom Fonda adores. When she leaves Guy Kibbee's circus for a better job, Fonda marries her replacement, Linda Darnell. Later, Fonda fights with Darnell and has a rendezvous with Lamour, but Lamour sends him away because she believes that he really loves his wife. Although it was anticipated to be a moneymaker, *Chad Hanna* did little at the box office.

Fortunately for Lamour, things picked up again when she filmed the second "Road" picture, *Road to Zanzibar* (1941, Paramount).

Right after *Road to Zanzibar*, Lamour played straight lady to Bob Hope in *Caught in the Draft* (1941, Paramount). Lamour plays the colonel's daughter, the object of movie star Hope's desire, but Hope cannot win her love unless he displays his patriotism by joining the army and becoming a hero. The obvious slapstick service comedy proved that Lamour was becoming more adept at playing farce. She also sang a song in the picture.

The Technicolor *Aloma of the South Seas* (1941, Paramount) reunited her with Jon Hall. Lamour does a number, and, for war-weary audiences, *Aloma of the South Seas* was for the most part a pleasurable night at the movies.

The Fleet's In (1942, Paramount) had woman-shy William Holden being photographed kissing dance-hall beauty Lamour in a publicity pose. The admiral's coy daughter, Barbara Britton, demands that Holden persuade Lamour to come to a party she is giving. Holden's shipmates take bets on the outcome, and the film eventually ends with Holden and Lamour linked romantically.

Although Lamour had top billing, *The Fleet's In* served more as a buildup for Betty Hutton, who, in tandem with comedy lead Eddie Bracken, proved to be the film's big drawing attraction.

Beyond the Blue Horizon (1942, Paramount) showcased Lamour as Tama, who is deserted on a tropical island when her parents are killed by a rampaging elephant during a hunting expedition. Lamour grows up with a domesticated chimpanzee and a tiger as her only companions. Eventually she is rescued and brought back to San Francisco to claim the inheritance that her parents left her, but when her authenticity is disputed, she leads a safari back to the Malayan island. Amidst the turmoil she falls for Richard Denning and still has time to vocalize a couple of songs in this standard movie fare.

Lamour's next feature was Paramount's third "Road" picture. *Road to Morocco* (1942, Paramount) enhanced Lamour's strong position in the Paramount star firmament but added little to her screen personality.

Lamour then made a guest appearance in *Star Spangled Rhythm* (1942, Paramount). This was at a time when almost all the studios were developing all-star extravaganzas wrapped around a thin story line concerning servicemen. United Artists released one called *Stage Door Canteen*; Warner Brothers produced two such pictures, *Thank Your Lucky Stars* and *Hollywood Canteen*; MGM had *As Thousands Cheer*; and Paramount's contribution was *Star Spangled Rhythm*. In this film, Paulette Goddard, Lamour, and Veronica Lake perform a song called "A Sweater, a Sarong, and a Peekaboo Bang" in which they spoof their respective screen trademarks.

On loan to Samuel Goldwyn, Lamour and Bob Hope appeared

in the slow-moving *They Got Me Covered* (1943, RKO). Hope plays an award-winning foreign correspondent who is fired by his news agency. He returns to Washington and tries to win his job back, but instead he gets the agency's star secretary and his girlfriend (Lamour) in some mild shenanigans as he inadvertently breaks up a spy ring. In this film, Lamour looked a bit bewildered and had no numbers to sing.

The Technicolor costume musical *Dixie* (1943, Paramount), set in pre–Civil War New Orleans, claimed to be the biography of Dan Emmett, composer of the title tune and many others.

Bing Crosby, as Emmett, weds his hometown sweetheart, Marjorie Reynolds. To prove his worth to her sullen father, Crosby sets out to become a success. Working on a riverboat, Crosby and Billy De Wolfe team up to form a minstrel act, and at Raymond Walburn's theatrical boardinghouse, Crosby is smitten with Walburn's daughter, Lamour. Once he has produced his innovative revue, however, she convinces him to return to the now crippled Reynolds. Lamour was easily lost in the shuffle of this film. Her only singing was in the ensemble finale number, "Dixie."

In her third 1943 release, *Riding High* (Paramount), Lamour plays Ann Castle, an ex–burlesque queen who returns home to Arizona when her show closes. Her father (Victor Moore) has fouled up his silver mine deal, and mining engineer Dick Powell has trouble refinancing the operation. Lamour goes to work as an entertainer at Cass Daley's dude ranch to earn her keep. Eventually, both the silver mine and the Powell/Lamour romance pan out.

And the Angels Sing (1944, Paramount) again teams Lamour with Betty Hutton as they play singing sisters who become intertwined in the life of shifty bandleader Fred MacMurray. He adroitly relieves the girls of $190 and then heads to New York. They follow him there, and as the story unfolds, each sister expresses a desire to pursue other goals. Their father (Raymond Walburn), fate, and love change their minds, however. Lamour performs a dance number with Frank Faylen, sings a song, and wins MacMurray. It was the effervescent singing of Hutton in *And the Angels Sing* that garnered the most public attention, however.

Rainbow Island (1944, Paramount) is an obvious Technicolor spoof of the waning sarong cycle. Lamour plays Lona, a white girl brought up on the Pacific island by her doctor father. Merchant marines Barry Sullivan, Eddie Bracken, and Gil Lamb make a forced landing on the island while escaping from the Japanese. Only because Bracken resembles a native god are the white men spared from sacrificial death. Only one of the four songs in the film is sung by Lamour.

In John Steinbeck's *A Medal for Benny* (1945, Paramount), Lamour received another chance to perform a straight dramatic role. Benny, one of the guys she finds herself "between," is never seen in the picture. Lamour is engaged to him, but after he joins the army, she finds out that he is a ne'er do well. Disillusioned, she turns to Joe, played by Arturo De Cordova, and falls in love with him. Just as they are ready to tell everyone, bad old Benny wins a posthumous medal for killing 100 Japanese. In this film, it was J. Carrol Naish as Benny's father who received the best critical notices.

In the all-star *Duffy's Tavern* (1945, Paramount), based loosely on the radio show of the same name, Lamour was on hand long enough to join Betty Hutton, Diana Lynn, Bing Crosby, and Arturo De Cordova in a satire on the song "Swinging on a Star."

In *Masquerade in Mexico* (1945, Paramount), Lamour is a stranded entertainer who is hired by Mexican banker Patric Knowles to portray a Spanish countess. The idea was for Lamour to lure matador Arturo De Cordova away from Knowles's straying wife, Ann Dvorak. Nothing much came of this film.

Fortunately, Lamour then made *Road to Utopia* (1945, Paramount). The film was completed in 1944 but was not released until December 1945 because of the backlog of movies produced during the lucrative war period.

In 1947, Lamour's last year under contract at Paramount, the sarong songstress had four major releases, although all in a costarring capacity.

Paired with Bob Hope again in *My Favorite Brunette* (1947, Paramount), Lamour plays an affluent heroine who is trying to locate her kidnapped uncle and is holding a map which pinpoints the location of valuable mineral deposits. She enters Alan Ladd's private detective agency and mistakes baby photographer Hope for an investigator. She convinces Hope to take the case as crooks Charles Dingle, Peter Lorre, and Lon Chaney, Jr., scramble to get to the mineral deposits first. Lamour sings one song in the picture.

Variety Girl (1947, Paramount), another 1940s all-star revue, features Lamour and Alan Ladd in the production number "Tallahassee." Their scene opens in an airplane where tough guy Ladd orders the pilot to land at gunpoint. Then he backs into the passenger cabin and breaks into song with stewardess Lamour.

In *Wild Harvest* (1947, Paramount), Lamour is the voluptuous seductress married to Robert Preston but in love with honorable Alan Ladd. No one's career was bolstered by this burdensome account of tempers erupting on the Western plains.

Road to Rio (1947, Paramount) redeemed Lamour with her public. It was becoming apparent that many of her fans preferred seeing her in roles that exhibited a tongue-in-cheek treatment of her love goddess position.

The mid–1940s brought a turning point in Lamour's career. Paramount decided that many of the company's expensive stars could be let go, and only Paulette Goddard and Betty Hutton were kept under contract. Lamour, Veronica Lake, Joan Caulfield, and others were axed. Dorothy Lamour then went into freelance work, using her past reputation as a star to carry her through mostly mediocre roles and minor films.

In 1948 she appeared in a multi-episodic failure called *On Our Merry Way* (1948, United Artists). In the second vignette, she plays an aspiring starlet and Victor Moore portrays a silent film era has-been. She sang one song in the film.

Lulu Belle (1948, Columbia), set in the 1900s, traces the life of Natchez-bred Lamour. She marries attorney George Montgomery, has a fling with prizefighter Gregg McClure, flirts with his manager Albert Dekker, and then goes to New York with millionaire Otto Kruger to become a stage star. Later she is shot; the rest is an uninteresting whodunit. Lamour did, however, perform five songs in the film.

Her other 1948 release was even more dismal. *The Girl from Manhattan* (1948, United Artists) casts her as a New York model returning home to find that her uncle (Ernest Truex) has mortgaged his boardinghouse to the limit. Lamour becomes involved with preacher George Montgomery and Bishop Charles Laughton. The final product has few redeeming entertainment qualities.

In 1949 Lamour appeared in *Manhandled* (Paramount). As secretary to phony psychiatrist Harold Vermilyea, Lamour becomes implicated in the murder of patient Alan Napier's wife, Irene Hervey. Lamour's involvement is furthered by her connections with boardinghouse neighbor and louse Dan Duryea. It takes insurance investigator Art Smith and some plot contriving to solve the crime and mercifully end the film.

Also in 1949, Lamour appeared in *The Lucky Stiff* (1949, United Artists). She plays nightclub singer Anna Marie St. Claire, who has supposedly been executed for murdering her employer. In reality, this sham execution is attorney Brian Donlevy's ploy to smoke out the suspects in the homicide case. Marjorie Rambeau as a fussy old client and Claire Trevor as Donlevy's long-suffering secretary took the few acting honors. Lamour performed one song.

Slightly French (1949, Columbia) is an above average film in which Lamour appears as Mary O'Leary, an Irish dancer at a carnival whom film director Don Ameche transforms into an exotic French import named Rochelle Olivia. Lamour sang two numbers in this motion picture.

As a favor to Bing Crosby, Lamour made a brief guest appearance playing herself in his starring vehicle *Here Comes the Groom* (1951, Paramount). In an airplane sequence, she, Louis Armstrong, Cass Daley, and Phil Harris join Crosby in singing "Misto Christofo Columbo."

In 1952, Cecil B. DeMille cast Lamour in the role of Phyllis, the aerialist who swings from a wire with a bit in her teeth, in *The Greatest Show on Earth* (Paramount). On the ground she offers advice and encouragement to fellow performers Betty Hutton and Gloria Grahame. The spectacle of the big top itself, however, drew more attention than any of the performers in the film.

Dorothy Lamour was considered a must when Bing Crosby and Bob Hope made their sixth "Road" feature, *Road to Bali* (1952, Paramount). After *Bali*, she did no film acting for nearly ten years and then made the seventh and final film of the "Road" series, *The Road to Hong Kong* (1962, Paramount).

In John Ford's adventure yarn *Donovan's Reef* (1963, Paramount), set in northern Hawaii, Lamour took sixth billing as Fleur, a Mae West type. For the most part, she remains on the sidelines while John Wayne and Lee Marvin slug it out. Elizabeth Allen wins Wayne, and Lamour eventually lands Marvin.

Lamour next turned up in the low-budgeted teenage musical film *Pajama Party* (1965, American International), playing a saleswoman in a dress store. Between the mild shenanigans and vocalizing of Tommy Kirk and heroine Annette Funicello and the lowbrow comedy of Elsa Lanchester and Buster Keaton, Lamour warbled a brief song and performed a few dance steps.

In 1987, Lamour was part of three vignettes based on Stephen King short stories in the film *Creepshow 2* (1987, Laurel/New World). *Creepshow 2* was a sequel to *Creepshow*, a more successful 1982 film.

In the vignette *Ol' Chief Wooden Head*, Lamour and George Kennedy play Martha and Ray Spruce, a sweet Southwestern couple running a general store in a small desert town. When the two are murdered, a cigar-store Indian, played by Dan Kamin, comes to life to avenge their murders. Lamour dies in the film almost before audiences are able to recognize her. The movie lacked any real chills or excitement and was nothing more than another unsuccessful attempt to turn Stephen King stories into film.

Lamour made more than 50 films in her career and for the years between 1936 and 1947, she was moviedom's prime South Seas maiden, laying claim to the title of cinema's first lady of the sarong. Lamour died in September 1996 at the age of 81, but because of those early films, she and her faithful sarong outfit continue as American institutions.

Bibliography

Burr, Lonnie. *Two for the Show: Great Comedy Teams*. New York: Julian Messner, 1979.

Crosby, Bing. *Call Me Lucky*. New York: Simon and Schuster, 1953.

Cross, Robin. *The Big Book of "B" Movies*. New York: St. Martin's, 1981.

_____. *2,000 Movies of the 1940s*. New York: Arlington House, 1985.

Eames, John. *The Paramount Story*. New York: Crown, 1985.

Faith, William Robert. *Bob Hope: A Life in Comedy*. New York: G. P. Putnam's Sons, 1982.

Furmanek, Bob, and Ron Palumbo. *Abbott and Costello in Hollywood*. New York: Perigee Books, 1991.

Giannetti, Louis D. *Understanding Movies*. Englewood Cliffs, N.J.: Prentice-Hall, 1972.

Green, Stanley. *Encyclopedia of the Musical Film*. New York: Oxford University Press, 1981.

Hemming, Roy. *The Melody Lingers On*. New York: Newmarket, 1986.

Hirschhorn, Clive. *The Hollywood Musical*. New York: Crown, 1981.

Hope, Bob, with Melville Shavelson. *Don't Shoot, It's Only Me*, New York: G. P. Putnam's Sons, 1990.

_____, with Pete Martin. *Have Tux, Will Travel*. New York: Simon and Schuster, 1954.

_____, and Bob Thomas. *The Road to Hollywood: My 40-Year Love Affair with the Movies*. Garden City, N.Y.: Doubleday, 1977.

Kanin, Garson. *Together Again!* Garden City, N.Y.: Doubleday, 1981.

Lamour, Dorothy, with Dick McInnes. *My Side of the Road*. Englewood Cliffs, N.J.: Prentice-Hall, 1980.

McNeil, Alex. *Total Television*. New York: Penguin Books, 1991.

Marx, Arthur. *Everybody Loves Somebody Sometime (Especially Himself)*. New York: Hawthorn Books, 1974.

_____. *The Secret Life of Bob Hope*. New York: Barricade Books, 1993.

Marx, Groucho, and Richard L. Anobile. *The Marx Bros. Scrapbook*. New York: Darien House, 1973.

Morella, Joe, Edward Z. Epstein, and Eleanor Clark. *The Amazing Careers of Bob Hope*. New Rochelle, N.Y.: Arlington House, 1973.

Nash, Robert Jay, and Stanley Ralph Ross. *The Motion Picture Guide*. Chicago: Cinebooks, 1986.

Parish, James Robert. *The Paramount Pretties*. New Rochelle, N.Y.: Arlington House, 1972.

Shepherd, Donald, and Robert F. Slatzer. *Bing Crosby: The Hollow Man*. New York: St. Martin's, 1981.

Siegel, Scott, and Barbara Siegel. *American Film Comedy*. New York: Prentice Hall General Reference, 1994.

Sinyard, Neil. *Classic Movie Comedians*. New York: Brompton Books, 1992.

Slide, Anthony. *The Encyclopedia of Vaudeville*. Westport, Conn.: Greenwood, 1994.

Steinberg, Cobbett. *Film Facts*. New York: Facts on File, 1980.

Thomas, Bob. *The One and Only Bing*. New York: Grosset & Dunlap, 1977.

Thompson, Charles. *Bing*. New York: David McKay, Inc., 1975.

_____. *Bob Hope: Portrait of a Superstar*. New York: St. Martin's, 1981.

Ulanov, Barry. *The Incredible Crosby*. New York: McGraw-Hill, 1948.

Index